fOMO
MARKETING TO MILLENNIALS

SUMEET SINGH LAMBA

EDITED BY ABHINAV SHARMA

CO-EDITED BY GURSHEEK KAUR

INDIA · SINGAPORE · MALAYSIA

Notion Press

No. 8, 3rd Cross Street,
CIT Colony, Mylapore,
Chennai, Tamil Nadu – 600 004

First Published by Notion Press 2021
Copyright © Sumeet Singh Lamba 2021
All Rights Reserved.

ISBN 978-1-63633-678-7

This book has been published with all efforts taken to make the material error-free after the consent of the author. However, the author and the publisher do not assume and hereby disclaim any liability to any party for any loss, damage, or disruption caused by errors or omissions, whether such errors or omissions result from negligence, accident, or any other cause.

While every effort has been made to avoid any mistake or omission, this publication is being sold on the condition and understanding that neither the author nor the publishers or printers would be liable in any manner to any person by reason of any mistake or omission in this publication or for any action taken or omitted to be taken or advice rendered or accepted on the basis of this work. For any defect in printing or binding the publishers will be liable only to replace the defective copy by another copy of this work then available.

To my son, Degveer

who is perpetually in FOMO.

Disclaimer

The author has made every reasonable effort to credit the source of material in this book. Any errors or omissions should be notified in writing to the author, who will endeavour to rectify the situation for any reprints and future editions. The copyrights of the credited source rest with the copyright/ source owners.

Contents

Acknowledgements   7
About the Book   11

1. Introduction   13
2. The Alchemy of FOMO   21
3. Millennials   33
4. Selling Fear, FOMO Style   51
5. Marketing to Millennials   69
6. Crafting FOMO in Marketing Strategy   81
7. Case Studies   109
   - The Binge Trap – Netflix   109
   - Influencer Marketing Strategy – Daniel Wellington   124

Epilogue   131
Notes   135
About the Author   141

Acknowledgements

The Covid-19 pandemic has brought up a period of unprecedented challenges for all of us. The ensuing lockdown in India commenced on March 25, 2020, forcing everyone to lock themselves up in their homes. At the same time, it opened my mind to a new range of possibilities. With more quiet time at hand, I introspected that marketers like myself are forever in a quest. They are forever in search of innovative methods to attract customers' attention. What could be some new triggers to compel customers to desire and eventually purchase a product or service? This question set me thinking. Researching and exploring, I stumbled upon the concept of FOMO and its impact on Millennial consumers.

Acknowledgements

The journey of this book from just a rudimentary idea to a rough draft and finally, the published copy could not have been complete without help and support from numerous people, whom I feel indebted to.

Family always comes first. Without the love and support of my parents, Jagdeep Singh Lamba (father) and Asha Lamba (mother), my brother Parmeet, my wife Gurpreet and son Degveer, this book would not have come about. Gurpreet had the unenviable job of acting as a whiteboard - listening to the rough drafts, vague ideas and progress reports, still appearing to be interested and encouraging, motivating me while keeping pace with her personal and professional commitments. Thank you, it surely would not have been possible without you or your endless supply of strong brew coffee.

Special mentions are in order for two people without whom this book would definitely not have seen the light of the day. The first one is a brilliant marketing professional and my close friend Abhinav Sharma, to whom I am indebted for his skilful editing. Over the past few months, he took out time from his busy schedule, challenging assumptions and making valuable suggestions to shape the content and readability of this book. The second is Gursheek Kaur, Assistant Professor, Post Graduate Department of English, Sri Guru Gobind Singh College, Chandigarh who generously gave her time and energy to go through this book time and again, correcting the flow and proof-reading it to give it a final shape, even though marketing is not quite her field of work. Most importantly, I thank them for oodles of patience they had to exhibit while working with me.

Special thanks to Vivek Sharma, who worked on the graphs and images in this book. Vivek was onboard the project the moment I requested his support. My deepest gratitude to him, who not only worked swiftly in giving the images a visual appeal but ensured that they complement the subject matter alongside.

I am also indebted to my extended family members especially, Dr TS Lamba, Sona Sethi, Jasjeet Singh Katial and Harmani Sethi who provided feedback on the initial draft and provided me with all the support to make this book a reality and a better read.

Thank you, everyone!

About the Book

Fear of Missing Out is a phenomenon as old as humanity itself, that has reached a tipping point amongst the Millennials. This shift has been fuelled by the newest form of communication – Social Media. As the battle for capturing customers' attention shifts from the physical to the digital arena, FOMO grows in its importance for marketers.

With a quarter of the population of the United States and one-third of India's population, 'Millennials' have become a mainstay of modern-day consumerism. Owing to sheer numerical strength, they currently exert a more substantial economic influence than any other generation alive, hence deserving today's marketers' attention.

About the Book

Brands and businesses today struggle to find innovative ways of reaching out to Millennials. Featuring numerous case studies and examples from across business models and industries, this book endeavours to enrich marketers' understanding of Millennials' digital lives and provide workable tips on the use of FOMO in marketing to capture the Millennial mind.

Useful for students of marketing, entrepreneurs and seasoned marketers alike, this book intends to suggest novel approaches to promote, position and place using one of the most potent marketing trends in the 21st century – FOMO!

» CHAPTER 1 «

Introduction

FOMO: We are in the midst of a FOMO epidemic. For the uninitiated, that is "Fear of Missing Out".

The concept of FOMO was introduced in the year 2000 in academic circles by marketing strategist Dr Dan Herman in an article titled "Introducing short-term brands: A new branding tool for a new consumer reality" published in the *Journal of Brand Management*. He illustrated the FOMO experience as the one based on the fear of – 'what will I miss because I do not have the necessary time or money, or because I do have another barrier of some kind?'.

The term FOMO found its way into the Oxford English Dictionary in the year 2013. Today, the acronym is infiltrating vocabularies across age-groups, locations and contexts. FOMO happens while one surfs through fashion blogs, travel podcasts, scans through lifestyle magazines or comes upon event invites. It happens when friends text their plans for the upcoming extended weekend to Goa. It can also get triggered by photos from a college classmate's latest beach vacation or by a colleague's tweet from the stand-up comic performance which one had to miss due to an upcoming office deadline. Inhabitants of the 21st century showcase an unparalleled awareness of what is "trending" and "in vogue", which makes them increasingly vulnerable to experiencing FOMO.

FOMO often emerges as a troubling feeling, a sense of anxiety triggered in response to events external to oneself. It mainly emanates from an apprehension that interest-worthy events are happening all around and one's peers are enjoying them in their absence. This initial feeling of anxiety and envy amplifies into self-doubt and even self-loathing.

Although caused by events far away, FOMO can have very tangible consequences closer home. Peaceful evenings in the living room can turn into panic sessions triggered by the constant flow of images and check-ins on one's social media newsfeed. While one browses through the latest fashion trends, new cafes and hip bars in town, it becomes concomitant that they feel left out of the parties, the gossip and the thrill of being present there at the moment.

The Curse of Connectivity

Today everyone is inundated with information about what is happening around them, about other people's affairs, and it does not help that all this information is available instantly at one's fingertips. Friends and peers do not help either; they flaunt all their FOMO-worthy moments on social media in real-time, ensuring that others see it, even against their volition.

According to Greek mythology, Argus Panoptes was a hundred eyed giant. His name Panoptes meant "the all-seeing one". Invocations of twenty-first century technology have summoned Argus from the myths into mundane daily lives, reincarnating as social media. Wherever one goes, whatever one does, there is just no hiding from being connected, continually experiencing the jitters of FOMO.

Like a modern-day Argus, social media forces everyone to see the constant happenings around them, making it harder to feel good about one's own choices. It is a classic case of food looking better at the adjoining table in a restaurant. No matter what one orders, there would still be something that will catch the eye as a more interesting option. Whether at home, during the daily commute or even at the dinner table with family, constant social media notifications haunt their users with the glimpses of eventful evenings they might have had, had they stepped out.

FOMO summarises an increasingly evident phenomenon – an ageless concept that has now reached a tipping point. From the perspective of evolutionary psychology, FOMO is a primaeval fear, being triggered by the newest form of communication, the Social Media. In the savannah of ten millennia earlier, getting left behind one's tribe could have meant likely death. Facebook, Twitter, Instagram, Snapchat, TikTok – all these are just modern weapons in the battlefield of the hunter gatherer's persevering psyche.

While bringing people closer than ever before, social media also broadens the scope for comparison with other's lives and experiences. Humans have never before experienced such a detailed insight into the lives of others. The immaturity of society's relationship with technology is evident from the uncontrollable bouts of scrolling social media feeds and being continually connected to gadgets. The Fear of Missing Out gets amplified by the combined effect of perpetual connectivity and ubiquity of technology.

The impact of FOMO induced by social media is most visible in Millennials, who are constantly glued to their smartphone screens. A generation of digital natives by birth, social media has become their community lifeline and a window to the world.

As FOMO increasingly becomes a reality of modern-day living, with its own set of triggers and characteristics, marketers would do well to decode and utilise it while reaching out to target consumers. While this book discusses the concept of FOMO largely in the context of social media and digital lives of modern-day customers, it undoubtedly stimulates and influences real-world behaviour too. As FOMO is here to stay, the brands seeking to engage and influence customers need to wake up to this essential way of attracting attention and initiating engagement.

New "Fear" on the Block

As noted earlier, the first academic paper on FOMO (Fear of Missing Out) was authored by Dr Dan Herman, back in the year 2000. His research began in 1996 when he observed FOMO as a phenomenon while interacting with customers talking about various products at focus groups or during interviews conducted for his study.

Across discussions on various product categories, one thing was strikingly similar – customers feared the thought of not being able to buy or experience exciting things that their peers had the chance to. Dr Herman found this to be a new development in consumer psychology and continued to research FOMO as a socio-cultural trend. Yet, it took another decade and a half for FOMO to capture marketers' attention and be given any serious thought.

The term FOMO owes its existence to Patrick McGinnis. In 2004, he wrote a piece for *The Harbus*, the newspaper of Harvard Business School, titled "Social Theory at HBS: McGinnis' Two FOs", which he identified as Fear of Better Options (FOBO) and Fear of Missing Out (FOMO).

McGinnis, in his light-hearted article for the newspaper, noted that students, because of their heavily loaded schedule struggled with a lot of things they aspired to finish or be a part of. Not only academic commitments, even keeping up with social commitments turned out to be stressful. In his 2004 article, McGinnis mentions, "FOMO led to a state of over-commitment in which people packed a single evening with nearly a dozen events, from Sherry tasting, to cocktails, dinners, parties, and after-parties, with the night culminating in a drunken email at three in the morning to a jilted friend: "Sorry I missed your 80's theme party at Felt—you know that you are totally in my top 15." However, having once been burned by missing an awesome event, one was likely to become hesitant to committing to anything for certain, leading to FOBO: the Fear of Better Options".[1]

Forces Behind the Rise

While the term itself was gaining currency, several social and technological forces were paving the path for the growth and spread of FOMO. In 2004, Facebook was an upstart adversary to Myspace with a minuscule number of users, growing steadily. The rise of Facebook and other social media along with the widespread use of smartphones and high-speed mobile internet access served as a fuel to the spread of FOMO. As a result, FOMO soon became a symbol of the digital age.

By 2007, newspapers and magazines had caught on with this term with *BusinessWeek* coming out with an article announcing that a FOMO epidemic was spreading rapidly. The desire to take part in all available social get-togethers, even if it involved a return trip from another part of the country or continent, drove students to blow up an enormous amount of money living these socially active and grandiose ways of life.

Subsequently, *The Guardian* included the term in its glossary of youth internet slang. By 2010, the term FOMO was being used and spoken of frequently and was invariably linked to social media usage.

The potential of FOMO as a marketing tool was eventually accepted by JWT Intelligence's trend report of March 2012. It highlighted how FOMO is triggered in teenagers and young adults, while also looking at its wide-ranging potential for brands seeking to leverage it to target consumers. FOMO was now in the limelight as a phenomenon that brands could take advantage of in their marketing strategy.

The Oxford dictionary defines FOMO as the "anxiety that an exciting or interesting event may currently be happening elsewhere, often aroused by posts seen on social media".[2]

Each generation has its buzzwords. Like the anti-war protests of USA in the 1970s and liberalisation debates in the 1990s in India, FOMO is soon becoming a global hallmark of the new age.

» CHAPTER 2 «

The Alchemy of FOMO

It is human nature to compare one's lives with those of others consistently. FOMO prompts an impulsive want to remain associated with others' experiences. Essentially, FOMO is a psychological term that points to one's innate need of never having to be left out. Social media and the constant need to remain connected with others has spawned an addiction to be up-to-date with the latest news and trends.

Factors Driving FOMO

FOMO emanates from a variety of sources, particularly from lifestyles and media habits of the 21st century. In order to utilise FOMO, in one's marketing campaigns, it is imperative to understand factors causing it first.

The Silicon Trap

Today 3.5 billion people use a smartphone daily accounting for 45% of the world's population. With a screen time of 30 hours in a week[1], smartphones are occupying people's visual space like no technology before. Having become a natural companion, the smartphones constantly crave the users' attention through notifications, alerts and reminders.

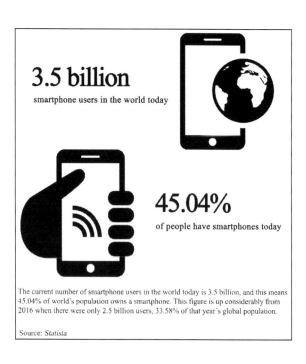

3.5 billion
smartphone users in the world today

45.04%
of people have smartphones today

The current number of smartphone users in the world today is 3.5 billion, and this means 45.04% of world's population owns a smartphone. This figure is up considerably from 2016 when there were only 2.5 billion users, 33.58% of that year's global population.

Source: *Statista*

Like, Share, Retweet – Repeat!

Social media assumes an increasingly significant role in the majority of people's lives. Close to 3 billion people globally have a profile on at least one of the many social media platforms, whether it is Facebook, Twitter, Instagram, Wechat, Reddit or TikTok.

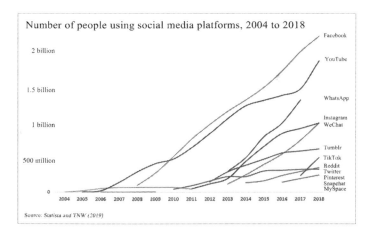

On the one hand, social media keeps everyone associated with their old friends while also allowing them to connect with new people. Also, it tends to be an incredible hotspot for learning new things, finding engaging videos or images, and following the latest news and trends. On the other hand, social media puts up the illusion that everyone except oneself is getting fitter, prettier, happier and wealthier. That is some information one may not be able to process or digest. When one looks at other people's high points chronicled on social media and compares them with the mundane living room reality that they find themselves ensnared in, it invariably pushes them towards pity or remorse.

If social media is anything to go by, one would surely think people are living their best lives. Comparing it with one's not so extraordinary life, generates the sentiment of FOMO. On a closer analysis, however, the people one envies may not be so "fab" themselves. They might have been stung by the same bug of FOMO; being themselves, a victim of previously generated FOMO. Everyone has heard of social media sensations suffering from clinical depression, who even end up taking their own lives despite having millions of followers and a FOMO worthy profile.

While witnessing others' dazzling personal lives and interests online, people are unintentionally falling prey to social media gamesmanship resulting in an acute sense of missing out. The effect of social media generated FOMO can be extreme among younger users who consume it the most. 62% of Facebook users are below 34 years of age[2] and spend 38 minutes daily on the platform.[3]

Not only among the social media savvy generations, but FOMO is also makings its way up towards older generations as they start embracing smartphones and social media.

A Digital Glasshouse

Social media today is a glamourised version of *The Truman Show*[4], a fairy tale in which everyone is a knight-in-armour or a princess of the realm. Handy mobile devices are facilitating lives lived conspicuously, with every plate of food vying to be "insta-worthy" and every outing to be check-in appropriate. With high-speed 4G networks and 64 megapixels camera, people are clamouring to show and tell all as it is happening. The internet has become a relentless stream of real-time news, information, conversations, memes and images. The proliferation of mobile broadband access and affordable gadgets means there is a perpetual burgeoning of this data stream around the clock and at every location.

The digital glasshouse of today is slowly but surely culminating into a mass-cultural phenomenon, and boundaries between private lives and Instagram profiles are disappearing fast.

Social Media Envy

This one is the most widely recognised indicator of FOMO. Social media envy happens when people start comparing their lives and events with experiences of others and start feeling inferior. Thanks to social media, people are not only able to see and view the lives of the celebrities as they bare open their lives to their fans but also of their friends and peers. Social media gives an illusion of bringing people closer to them, but the reality is unfathomable by the majority.

Newsfeeds or Tweets that are more likely to intensify FOMO are not from Katrina Kaif or Dan Bilzerian but from one's peers – friends, schoolmates, colleagues or cousins. It is with them whom people compare their lives regularly, in a virtual duel in their minds and on social media.

Closet Stalking

Majority of the people have experienced a weird feeling when one's friends have decided to go and watch a movie or make that road trip which they all had planned together but were left behind. Having been left behind, one cannot but continuously eye their social media feed to check on all the action they have missed. People scan through different platforms to keep themselves updated on what others are doing, and in turn, delve deeper and deeper into FOMO.

FOMO is not only caused by the escapades of one's immediate circle of friends and peers, but also by one's kith and kin far away. Social media, in that sense, expands the horizons of FOMO and brings out the closet stalker in all of us.

Life in Overdrive

With a plethora of books to read, binge-worthy series releasing every other day on Amazon Prime, new fashion lines being launched by Zara and other fast fashion brands, people already have their plates full with too much to do, read, watch and shop. Every day, it is becoming harder than ever before to achieve all this without missing out on something.

The moment one decides to finish off the long-pending college project, a friend makes a plan for an instant birthday celebration at the neighbourhood pizza joint. At that instant, one gets torn between the task at hand and postponing it yet again, for the feeling of FOMO is too strong to fight.

#Hashtag Life

With the advent of indexed search, hashtags are the perfect labels for social media posts and a sure way to get noticed. Adding a hashtag to pictures and events, people across the globe are making their presence felt to everyone by telling them where they are and what they are up to. Hashtags are an excellent tool to bring attention to events, posts and products online. Following or searching a hashtag makes information about the exciting topics instantly available, ensuring one does not miss a thing about the topic at hand.

Engagements Using Hashtags on Different Social Media Platforms:

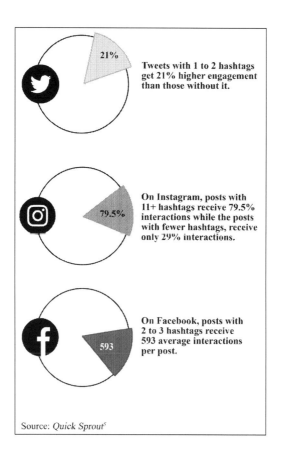

Source: *Quick Sprout*[5]

As modern lives become increasingly connected, and social media plays an even bigger role in day-to-day interactions, FOMO is an inevitable force which will govern social and buying behaviours. With the ever-expanding role of gadgets, automation and communication technologies, people will inevitably experience an increasing amount of FOMO in their day-to-day lives. Therefore, it becomes imperative that marketers understand and learn to harness FOMO to achieve their objectives, namely brand awareness and purchase decisions.

FOMO Addiction

Fear of Missing Out is a modern manifestation of the intrinsic human fear. Unlike in the ancient times, getting separated from one's tribe may not be a matter of life and death anymore, but one's brain is still wired to make a big deal out of it. In today's era, when social media has become a community lifeline, being left behind from the check-ins, photo-tags and @ mentions may evoke acute feelings of anxiety and isolation.

Millennials today exhibit an obsession towards being connected. They are often multitasking on their gadgets where one call gets interrupted to receive another and video calls are minimised to check the sender of the text on a group chat. Even on the work front, there are so many apps to "collaborate" and "share" in real-time that even a five-minute delay can give them jitters.

Holidays are no different. Even on a hike in the woods, one cannot resist searching for mobile networks just to check their Facebook and Twitter posts as if something better or more entertaining may happen right at the moment one steps out of their network coverage area.

Connecting through Facebook walls, Twitter streams, Instagram updates, and through LinkedIn refreshes, people today can hardly ever detach from anyone any longer. Ironically, getting out of the "information array" causes inexplicable stress; and that is what they wish to avoid by staying glued to their screens.

In an endeavour to avert the stress response from kicking in, some people, unfortunately, intensify their attempts to not miss out on anything by continuously refreshing their Facebook or Twitter feeds to see if they are missing out on anything. This results in getting stuck in a quagmire of addiction wherein not wanting to miss out on things results in the feeling of missing out even stronger.

People's relationship with technology is still nascent and rapidly evolving. With the legacy of social, psychological and emotional baggage accumulated over millions of years of evolution, one is yet to figure out how to interact well using technology. Studies on the sustained use of electronic, internet media impacting one's mental and social well-being are still inconclusive at best. Thus, it is a common sight to see one's parents struggling to keep up with relatives on WhatsApp or colleagues frantically refreshing their Outlook mails, sometimes with distressed looks on their faces. Across one's personal as well as professional lives, everyone is in the grip of "FOMO addiction".

Having been born in an era of internet ubiquity, teenagers today feel that technology is a natural extension of their lives. They continue to shape their lives around technology and the social connections that come with it, rather than the other way around. They stay up all night waiting for their friends' next status update. Few of them can carry out a face-to-face conversation with anyone without being distracted by the urge to check their smartphones to make sure that nothing better is going on somewhere else. The current social media apps earn their fortunes in direct proportion to the time spent by their users and the number of pages visited by them. It is this very feature of social media that compels its users to experience FOMO and drives them to keep checking on their social media applications more often than ever.

Exponential growth in the availability of social media applications and devices to access them round the clock has also resulted in a similar growth in anxiety levels.[6] One's device screen has become a window to envy, anxiety and yearning. Despite such consequences, media and technology giants have always found a way to keep them addicted to their FOMO machinery.

Understanding how and why FOMO is caused, brands are eager to convert these human feelings into buyer behaviour. FOMO is driving new diktats in marketing, and brands that can effectively tap into this feeling could very well find the key to influence purchase behaviours of their users.

» CHAPTER 3 «

Millennials

The term "Millennial" is being used more than ever in today's time. It appears in news articles, business magazines and is a part of everyday conversations centred around young adults and their choices in life.

The Millennial generation sometimes even courts controversy among economic studies and business articles for being a radically different generation than the ones before them.

Millennials also called the millennial generation, is the phrase used to usually describe persons or individuals who have reached adulthood in the early 21st century, generally covering people born between years 1980 and 2000. When the phrase started to take shape, many used to associate it with students who would graduate high school by the year 2000. The beginning and concluding birth years of the Millennials is a matter of varied debates and mixed opinions amongst many. Some researchers and publications identify the mid-1970s to early 90s as birth years of Millennials, while others use 2004 as the closing birth year. While there may still be a disagreement about who qualifies to be a Millennial, the broadly accepted version, is of an individual born after the 1980s till 2000.

As per the US archetype, Millennials, also known as Generation Y, are the demographic entity that immediately follows Generation X and is succeeded by Generation Z. A 2017 paper published by KPMG puts 1980 and 1995 as the margin years for the millennial generation.

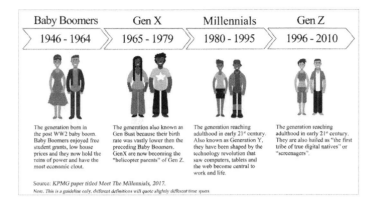

Source: *KPMG paper titled Meet The Millennials, 2017.*
Note: This is a guideline only, different definitions will quote slightly different time spans.

"Everyone is born unique" – is an oft-repeated humanist aphorism. However, specific environmental and cultural circumstances of any generation tend to influence individuals belonging to the same age-group. These easily noticeable, relatively homogenous groups tend to share similar wide-ranging propensities and predictable characteristics as consumers.

The Millennial DNA

Growing up at the turn of the Millennium and having witnessed large scale changes in social, political, economic and technological spheres, Millennials are different from their immediate predecessors Generation X (also known as the GenX or the MTV generation) in more ways than one.

Unlike GenX, Millennials were exposed to technology at a far younger age. Yet, both the generations seem to have adopted emerging technology trends with an open mind, albeit in their unique ways. Other shared qualities of both the generations are self-sufficiency and appreciation for work-life balance. Even so, Millennials exhibit many traits which are in complete contrast to the previous generation, often being touted as being too self-centred and overly reliant on technology.

Even across geographies, Millennials exhibit a set of similar traits, helping us distinguish them from other generations preceding and succeeding them. They are the most studied and discussed generation to date. They further happen to be the first generation that grew up with technology. Technology has helped them shape their identities, and this is a generation that cannot even imagine a world without the internet or smartphones.

Through millions of years of history, humans evolved to share their lives and stories in person or through the written word. However, Millennials prefer to communicate via text messages, email or social media platforms like Twitter, Facebook or Instagram, expressing opinions and stories through likes, comments, shares, upvotes and audio or video snippets. They consistently use these forms of communication to find jobs, cool outfits, even love interests or life partners. Millennials are skilled at understanding new digital interfaces and adapting to newer technologies as they come.

Seeking Roots

The Millennial generation has been at the epicentre of far-reaching social, political and especially, technological changes. Today's world is hardly recognisable from the world they grew up in. Wired telephones, VHS, gaming parlours, have all been replaced with gadgets and gizmos. This speedy transition and frequent evolution make it difficult for users to have an emotional connection with their devices.

Increasing urbanisation and development of new service and technology industries has led to mass exodus and resettlement of Millennials away from their roots. This movement has resulted in Millennials savouring anything connected to their childhood. This nostalgia for "good old times" has now emerged as a new selling proposition.

Everywhere, Everytime

Ever since Apple decided to foray into mobile computing by launching the iPhone, mobile phone capabilities and interfaces have never been the same. In current times, mobile technology is vital to Millennials in all fields of life and work. It not only helps them stay connected to their social circle or in entertainment pursuits, like playing games or watching online videos, it has also evolved into a primary method of learning, researching and forming opinions.

Majority of the Millennials graduated college and started entering the formal workforce at the height of the global economic recession in the late 2000s. As a result, the Millennials have much lesser in terms of real earnings, own fewer assets and savings compared to earlier generations at a similar age.

While it is essential to understand that all Millennials may not showcase the same personality traits, there are some commonly agreed characteristics which are frequently linked to the Millennials:

- Over-dependence on technology, especially mobile internet and social media
- Inclination towards spending money on brands or businesses with whose vision or mission they can associate themselves
- An aspiration to do work that carries a sense of fulfilment or accomplishment at a skill
- High attrition rate especially, in developing economies and technology-intensive sectors
- Celebrating and showcasing success no matter how big or small.

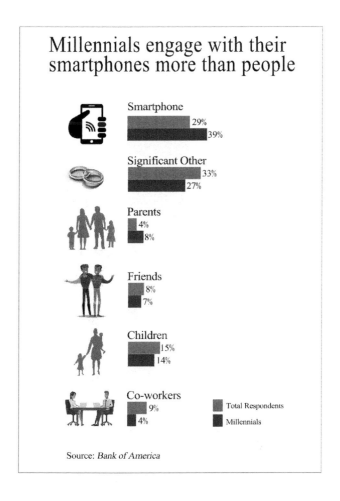

Deloitte's 8th annual Millennial Survey 2019 report revealed that faced with continuous societal and technological disruption, Millennials and Gen Zs seem disillusioned with traditional institutions, cautious of business objectives and pessimistic about the current economic and social progress. In general, given the growth and foreseeable potential of the world economy, the younger generations are far more sceptical of the world and their place in it as compared to any of their immediate predecessors.

Still, contrary to the world view, Millennials are no less ambitious. A substantial majority wants to earn high salaries and achieve professional success. However, their goals have changed and, in most cases, hindered by financial constraints. A person born in the 1960s in most countries would have considered having children, purchasing homes, retiring from one-job as the gold standard for a fulfilling life. Yet, these success parameters do not even apply to Millennials. Rather than accumulating money in pension funds and luxurious houses and cars, travelling and seeing the world is at the top of their list (57 per cent) while a little less than half (49%) said they wanted to buy a home.

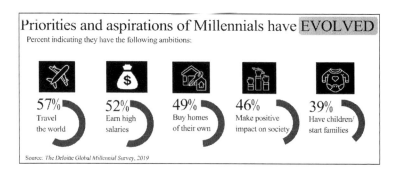

Interestingly, Millennials are more inclined towards making a positive impact in their communities or society at large (46 per cent) than to have kids and start their families (39 per cent).

Millennials generally though seem to be optimistic about their ambitions and goals being within their reach. Two-thirds of Millennials who aspired to climb up the corporate ladder to a high-ranking profile in their careers believed it was feasible. Seven out of ten who wanted to explore and travel the world thought it was possible. Even among Millennials who wished to purchase homes, the majority are optimistic that they would be able to.

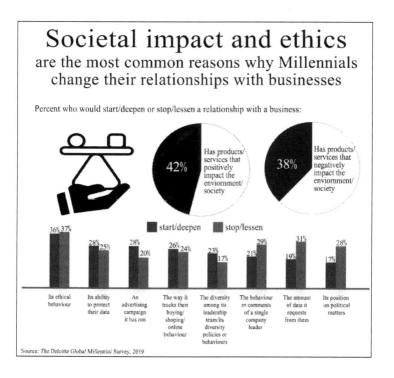

A Disruptive Generation

Millennials have fundamentally different consumption and ownership patterns as compared to their predecessors. As consumers, their actions and choices are significantly disrupting existing business and societal practices and shaking up established norms of doing business. Their attitude towards material goods like houses and apartments influence their buying decisions, where they prefer to lease or rent instead of owning.

It is not just the homes that the Millennials are not interested in buying. They are reluctant to purchase other goods and items like cars, music, furniture, luxury goods and clothes. Instead, they are veering towards a new set of service providers that provides them access to products and services they need without the obligation of owning them. It has resulted in the rise of a new type of economy called sharing economy characterised by a change from ownership to "usership".

Even in the workplace, Millennials exhibit novel trends, unlike any of the previous generations. Whereas, loyalty to the employer was the hallmark on which the modern capitalistic economy was built; on the other hand, Millennials are bereft of their allegiance towards anyone or anything. They do not hesitate to switch jobs at short notice if they are dissatisfied either with their pay, promotions or even their employers' stance on various social and environmental issues.

Facebook Employees Stage Virtual Walkout to Protest Trump Posts

While Twitter started labeling some of the president's inflammatory posts, Facebook's chief executive, Mark Zuckerberg, has said his company should leave them alone.

Source: *The New York Times*[1]

Life is a Gig

The emergence of outsourcing, contracting and "temp" workers for enhancing profitability and reducing employer liabilities has been a significant trend, especially in the decades since Millennials started joining the workforce.

The market based on freelance or short-term contract work, also known as the gig economy, offers short term engagements and quick mobility to both Millennials and businesses. The Millennials look forward to joining the gig economy for two primary reasons. One, for the chance to earn more money and second, to be able to work at the hours they prefer.

An illustration of the origins of this mindset goes back to the financial crisis of the late 2000s. This generation was raised in a time when they saw houses, cars and other material possessions belonging to their parents suddenly become a financial burden instead of a blessing. As a direct result of that recession, the concept of sharing economy found its wings and the movement from ownership to "usership" pattern started to take shape, especially amongst the young consumers.

Access, not ownership

It's not just homes: Millennials have been reluctant to buy items such as cars, music and luxury goods.

Instead, they are turning to a new set of services that provide access to products without the burdens of ownership, giving rise to what is being called a "sharing economy."

Source: Goldman Sachs Global Investment Research

A Shared World

As observed above, the millennial generation values experience more than the accumulation of material goods. In the case of necessities, such as accommodation and transportation, higher emphasis is placed on accessibility rather than on ownership. Purchasing a home is no longer a necessity, a life goal or even a symbol of financial security. Own less and experience more is the chant they follow.

The sharing economy or collaborative consumption has become the new normal. From housing to education and financial services, the sharing economy is steadily disrupting almost every industry traditionally controlled and operated by conventional large corporations.

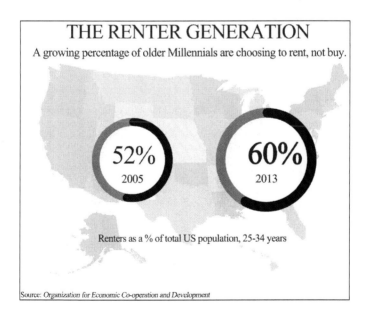

Such drastic changes in buying behaviour of Millennials have led to the rise of newer corporations and business models which are re-inventing the way business is done in the 21st century. The surge of technology-driven "usership focused" startups like Uber, Airbnb, Yulu, and WeWork are symbols of consumerism in the Millennial age. Even in leisure activities such as watching movies and listening to music, owning CDs and DVDs have been replaced with subscription-based services such as Netflix and Gaana. Such changes are forcing even existing companies to rethink their business models to adapt and survive with the Millennial expectations and the sharing economy.

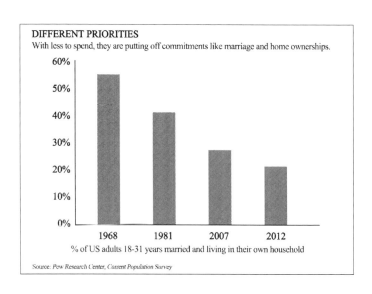

Bytes of Change

Headwinds in the economy have increased the stress on affordability. However, the Millennials' love for everything "here and now" has led to the emergence of new models of affordability which is integrally linked with convenience. Affordability and convenience have indeed become critical drivers for businesses today. The concept of renting and leasing is an age-old concept, but advancements in easily accessible technology have opened up new models for the sharing economy to blossom. Practices such as hyperlocal purchasing of products and services via GPS enabled smartphones and payments made from digital mobile wallets have become the mundane reality of everyday life. Emerging fields like Data Analytics, Big Data, Machine Learning and Artificial Intelligence have enabled sellers to identify idle capacity and fine-tune supply chains. It allows them to make the products and services available to the consumers at prices they are willing to pay, at places where they want.

Another novel trend which may set apart Millennials from any of the preceding generations is the concept of co-living. It has become the latest buzzword amongst Millennials, not just in western countries but in India as well. It offers an attractive alternate housing for the young generation who are looking for a solution to the urban housing problems.

The co-living service provider also takes care of requirements like furnishings, kitchen and upkeep facilities. Located close to business offices and designed efficiently, keeping in mind Millennials' fascination with convenience, co-living residences can help Millennials save on time, money and energy.

Another business model called subscription boxes has also been developed to cater to the Millennial generation. These are curated collections of items that are delivered at the doorstep of the customer periodically, usually monthly or quarterly. These can range from clothing items to cosmetic products and from organic or gluten-free food deliveries to indulgent goodie boxes for the Millennials. The combination of convenience, assortment, along with the fondness for surprises is fuelling the growth of subscription-based products.

A popular example of a subscription-based business is the Dollar Shave Club. Founded in 2011, in the USA, it delivers razors, blades and personal grooming products through online orders. Customers receive their subscription items via mail, direct to their homes, based on their preferences set on the website itself. Dollar Shave Club relies on subscription by the members as the primary mode of orders and home delivery rather than the traditional over-the-counter sale usually undertaken by the consumers.

Size Does Matter

The Millennial generation forms a quarter of the population of the United States, making them the largest living generation – the biggest in US history, more numerous than the Baby Boomers. In India, they make up close to one – third of the entire nation's population.

India's Millennials, 400 million and growing:

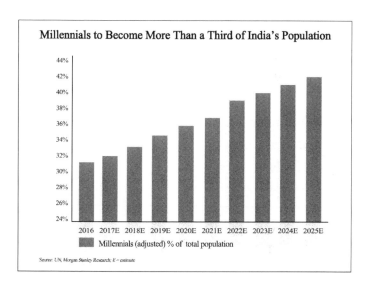

With such substantial population numbers, the Millennials are all set to take centre stage in the consumer markets as they reach their prime working and spending age. Their impact on the economy is also going to be huge as they redefine the consumption story by driving and dominating the entire consumer market.

The combination of factors discussed in this chapter has led to an overly engaged and continuously distracted breed of people. Many studies suggest that Millennials are the most stressed generation in history.[2] Unable to "disconnect" from anything, including their thoughts, their overexposure to so many happenings around them is taking a severe toll on their mental and social well being.

Caught in a continuous cycle of technological dependence, sleep deficiency and unrealistically high expectations set by the digital world, Millennials are suffering at the hands of the technologies they love the most. As a result of their demographic heft, and their current and future spending powers, marketers need to learn how to engage with Millennials. In such a situation, FOMO can help capture their attention.

» CHAPTER 4 «

Selling Fear, FOMO Style

As per marketing guru Dr Philip Kotler, *"Marketing is the science and art of exploring, creating, and delivering value to satisfy the needs of a target market at a profit. Marketing identifies unfulfilled needs and desires. It defines, measures and quantifies the size of the identified market and the profit potential. It pinpoints which segments the company is capable of serving best and it designs and promotes the appropriate products and services."* [1]

Essentially, a major part of marketing involves persuading the target audience to make a purchase, increase purchase frequency or expedite future purchases. Consumers base their purchasing behaviour on a complex web of habits, expectations, urges, motivations and biases. A marketer needs to reach out to segments which are most likely to purchase at a time and place where the influence on buying behaviour can be maximised.

Over the years, marketers have been striving to influence buying behaviour using an array of techniques and appeals. Among the various tools used by advertisers, fear has been one of the main ingredients. Fear works in marketing and advertising as it is an easily recognisable emotion that triggers people to change their behaviour and respond urgently. Fear has been the mainstay of advertising for products and services such as insurance, health and safety-related products such as sanitation and hygiene products, helmets and even mundane products such as toothpaste.

Another form of fear, associated with loss of reputation or feeling left out in one's social circle, can also be noted. While owning the latest PlayStation game or the latest AirPods may not be linked with physical well being or safety, many purchase decisions shall invariably be impacted by the fear of being left behind the social circle. A family may even choose to own or subscribe to products and services such as Netflix, a Golf club membership or a Google Home speaker purely out of the urge to stay in step with their neighbourhood.

While it is evident that fear spurs people towards a purchase, two essential factors govern how and why consumers feel anxiety:

1. **Vulnerability - "How likely would the scenario affect me?"**

The concept of vulnerability determines whether the product or service advertised has a relationship with the customer profile. The likelihood of making a purchase decision is directly proportional to the relatability of fear appeal used for marketing the product. Selling air purifiers to someone with young kids living in a metropolitan city using fear appeal would make more sense as compared to selling it to someone living in the countryside.

2. **Severity - "To what extent would it affect me?"**

Severity impacts the magnitude of the customer's response to a given marketing proposition. An area of concern which may seem remote to a customer may not be a critical lever in impacting customer behaviour. Marketing of term insurance to college students would have a far lesser impact than to middle-aged professionals with family liabilities.

Given the context of current market realities and consumer insights elaborated upon in previous chapters, fear in the form of FOMO emerges as a potent tool for marketers today. For the younger generations, especially Millennials, for whom social media and remaining connected with their social circle in their everyday life is a priority, the efficacy of using the Fear of Missing Out in marketing strategies can be remarkable.

A combination of tight work schedules, long commutes and overexposure to multiple media sources makes it almost impossible for a marketer to capture a Millennial's attention. It does not help that several studies have estimated this attention span to be just 12 seconds. Arousing FOMO through crisp messaging and appropriate imagery may form the holy grail of breaking the clutter and reaching out to Millennials.

The Secret Science of Creating FOMO

We have already established that since ages, human beings have suffered from this incessant desire to be "in the know" and be "in on the action". Understanding and leveraging this desire can be decoded using three principles of behavioural science which are being utilised by marketers today for inducing FOMO:

Creating Scarcity/ Limiting Availability

The prospect of losing out on a product when it is available in short supply, for a limited time or available on a first-come-first-serve basis only, can send consumers into a FOMO overdrive. Brands creating scarcity or urgency in consumers' minds by restricting the period of availability has been a time-tested marketing technique. "Limited stocks available" or "limited period deals" have been popular rallying cries which are utilised by brands to trigger a shopping frenzy. However, their real value is only being realised now, thanks to amplification through social media.

Putting constraints on availability or quantity will expedite purchases and may even cause panic buying, thereby increasing the expected demand for the product. Through online shopping events like End of Reason Sale, Great Online Shopping Festival, Cyber Monday and many more, online businesses have been able to leverage FOMO in unprecedented ways.

Booking.com, a popular online hotel accommodation booking website uses FOMO to create a sense of urgency in the minds of the customers who are on the lookout for a hotel room. A message in red coloured font warns us about deals that have been sold out or are in high demand with limited spaces available. By showing a limited number of accommodations available in the hotel the customer is interested in, they are effectively pushing the customer into considering booking that room soon enough lest they lose out on their preferred accommodation.

Screenshot Courtesy: Booking.com

Online retail giant, Amazon takes a similar approach with "Lightning Deals" and "Black Friday Sale" which have become a marquee feature of its shopping platform. These deals and sales exploit the scarcity principle cleverly, creating a sense of urgency in the consumer's mind. As the products appear to be in limited supply, customers are left wanting to purchase lest they run out of stock.

The marketing hype created around these events drives not only new enrolments and business volumes among excited potential customers, but it may also stimulate some customers to buy and hoard items they may or may not eventually use.

Another way of creating urgency to boost business outcomes is by offering curated, limited-time experiences on one's platform. CultFit, a fitness-focused Indian brand, offers workouts and dance classes with celebrities to augment subscriptions. Uber, the ride-hailing service offers heli-rides on a first-come-first-serve basis to a limited set of customers as part of its brand building and customer engagement efforts.

Social Proof

The web is a vast repository of information which can often be misleading and confusing. Since the internet has become the primary supplier and custodian of data on practically any topic today, most consumers feel a sense of bewilderment while making purchase decisions, whether online or even offline.

A plethora of information inundates a customer about products or services available in the market. This surfeit of information overwhelms a prospective buyer who may or may not have wanted the product or service offered. In either of the situation, the prospective buyer may be favourably motivated to make a purchase through peer generated ratings, reviews, testimonials and endorsements by influencers; which are considered to be authentic and relatable.

Social proof is the term given to the psychological phenomenon wherein people replicate others' behaviour in a particular situation to achieve similar objectives. The premise of social proof is that if a significant number of others have behaved in a specific way, it must be the correct behaviour. Social proof can give customers powerful emotional triggers that significantly influence their reaction and response to a brand or even to specific products. It not only helps them in choosing a product but also inspires confidence in their choices, alleviating post-purchase dissonance. Social proof can even justify premium pricing by authenticating performance or quality-related claims about the product.

Social proof demonstrates that other people are not just purchasing from the brand or utilising its services; they genuinely appreciate these so much that they are advocating it to the world. On the internet, social proof can be in the form of reviews or testimonials, ratings, or user-generated content, tagging a brand through their social media handle or appropriate hashtags referring to specific brands, events and emotions.

With the expansion of social media to various formats and platforms, people, especially Millennials, are sharing their likes and dislikes in more ways and more places than ever before. Photos, videos and check-ins document their daily life experiences often labelled with a hashtag. Vacations, movies, parties, dates and new purchases are all over people's social media feed, reinforcing social proof.

In such a connected world, marketers need more than just smart marketing content to lure audiences to dive into their brand. Social proof is the definitive means of promoting brand and product awareness reinforced with a sense of trust and authenticity. If appropriately utilised, social proof can convert customers into brand advocates or brand ambassadors more than any marketing campaign could.

As social media usage is widespread among the younger generation, adverse social proof can make or break a brand in today's time. If the IMDB ratings or Rotten Tomatoes approval score falls below a threshold level, for any movie or show, other people start getting dissuaded from watching it. Similarly, a low score on Zomato generally leads to consumers opting out from visiting a specific restaurant or skipping to order online from there.

Ratings and reviews on Google, Justdial, Zomato, Yelp, Amazon Reviews, Glassdoor and other such portals act as important gatekeepers between a brand and its prospective customers. Hobby or interest-specific online communities and forums like Lonely Planet, xBHP, Quora, Android Central have emerged as more authentic and relatable sources of information or support for current or future customers of a brand. These forums address not only the specifications or performance aspects of a product or service; they also give insights on user experience based on real-life tests, even updating customers on hacks and troubleshooting shortcuts.

Two recent examples of brands utilising social proof as an effective tool are HBO's promotional campaign for *Game of Thrones Season 8* and Smirnoff's "Be There" campaign.

HBO, an American cable television company, effectively leveraged FOMO for their super successful television series *Game of Thrones*. Ever since the ending of *Game of Thrones, Season 7,* HBO kept on leveraging their social channels keeping the audiences engaged with images and clips from its past seasons, building up nostalgia and generating expectations for an upcoming Season 8.

HBO, leveraging the *Game of Thrones* imagery, even partnered with a plethora of brands like Oreos, Bud Light, Mountain Dew and even American Red Cross. American Red Cross even went a step further by encouraging fans to commit to donating blood. These partnerships yielded positive hype for the HBO and *Game of Thrones* brand which kept the interest in the upcoming series alive while also exhibiting that it was purpose-driven.

The social media campaigns for the famous series made creative use of hashtags like #TakeTheThrone and #ForTheThrone to ensure consistent traction across social platforms. HBO was able to generate the right set of social proof across digital media from everyone, including the right brand partners and also through celebrity collaborations.

Image/ Post Credit: Twitter/ @RedCross

Smirnoff launched the "Be There" campaign with the Nightlife Exchange Project in the year 2011 which offered opportunities to their target audience to experience the nightlife and attend parties in cities around the globe. The FOMO-inducing campaign called out everyone with the question – When was the last time you said: "I was there"?

They incited customers to post ideas and pictures of their city's nightlife on their social media platform and encouraged everyone to vote for the best ideas. The best ones got turned into live events held across the world. Customers who submitted the winning concepts got selected to swap their nightlife event with someone from another part of the globe.

To make it more interesting, they also swapped the events; where a bright idea from Germany might turn out to be an event in Brazil while a Japanese submission may make its way up to Canada. Smirnoff even partnered with Madonna to further spike the audience's interest in these events. Encouraging dancers to submit their audition videos online, Madonna herself invited the best of the lot for the chance to dance with her.

The programme elicited a massive response across social media and Smirnoff's registered userbase. It's Facebook community grew by 375 per cent, making it the most prominent online community of any spirits brand at that time. Not just on social media, it earned media coverage in every market with press impressions for the project reaching over one billion worldwide.

All these thanks to a mind-boggling campaign revolving around the Millennial fear of not just someone saying, "You should have been there" but being there to experience it.

Image Courtesy: Smirnoff Ice "Be There" Promotional Campaign

Loss Aversion

Loss aversion is one of the most critical factors triggering FOMO. People generally tend to avoid losses than to make a profit. People tend to be more concerned with the prospect of losing out on something if they do not act rather than gaining something by taking timely and desirable action. In other words, "Do not miss out on this deal" will generate more awareness and response than "Take advantage of this deal".

A behavioural study by Nobel Laureates Daniel Kahneman and Amos Tversky explicitly posits that "the pain of losing is psychologically about twice as powerful as the pleasure of gaining".[2] Therefore, loss aversion often causes people to take prompt actions to avoid missing out on what they perceive as important.

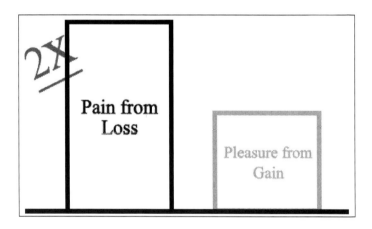

Successfully using loss aversion in marketing means precisely understanding what the customers are afraid of losing and why, and then providing them with a solution to avoid that loss. Language plays a very critical role in marketing with the use of FOMO to send the correct message and create the required urgency. Promoting what people may gain from a service is likely to yield fewer results than telling people what they are missing out on upon.

We can further understand the concept of loss aversion using the below examples of various marketing techniques deployed by brands.

Coupons – Coupons are a classic tactic that still works in the digital age. Coupons or vouchers trigger loss aversion far more forcefully than a regular sales promotion such as "upfront discounts" or "Buy One Get One (BOGO)". Unlike the "hypothetical" discounts which consumers would gain by making the purchase, not being able to utilise a voucher earned by them triggers the sense of losing out. A condition like this urges the customers to take swift action, unlike in sales promotions. To further amplify FOMO using coupons, brands sometimes put an expiry date on their vouchers; this additionally expedites buying decision since customers do not want to lose something valuable by not acting promptly.

Loyalty Points – Loyalty points offered by brands also operate on the principle of loss aversion. These points can be redeemed while making further purchases from the brand, either as a substitute for cash or for claiming gifts from the company catalogue. Having accumulated points on previous purchases motivates customers to stay loyal to the brand and frequently shop with them, thereby collecting more reward points in the process to keep the cycle going. To further increase customers' engagement, some brands increase the stakes by including milestone-based exclusive rewards. Since most loyalty points also come with an expiry date, the fear of losing out on those plays well with the psyche of the customers. Even for the newly acquired customers, some brands provide "Welcome Points" to ensure repeat purchase and generate loyalty.

Free Trials – Free trials operate on the concept of ownership, creating perceived emotional bonds with the customers by providing them short term or conditional ownership of a product or service. The prospect of losing this ownership can trigger loss aversion behaviour, thereby converting the trial into a purchase decision. Offering free trials of a brand gives a first-hand experience of benefits of ownership of the product or service while also nurturing a sense of potential loss when the trial period ends. Towards the end of the trial period, the thought of losing out on the benefits enjoyed during the trial period creates FOMO in the customer's mind. This results in creating a strong urge of buying the paid membership or subscription.

YouTube uses this loss aversion tactic extensively as an onboarding technique for its YouTube Premium service. A one-month free subscription of YouTube Premium costs nothing and is, therefore, a clear and easy proposition for the customer. However, the trial may highlight the benefits of premium subscription and trigger FOMO, resulting in the purchase of the subscription at the end of the trial period.

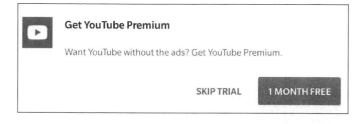

Screenshot Courtesy: YouTube

If one needs to utilise FOMO adequately, the benefits of acting at once ought to be the underlying message. Also, it needs to be crystal clear to the audience what they stand to miss out. A perfect example of this is when at the time of the launch of a new flagship product, few of the popular mobile handset brands offer exclusive rewards when consumers pre-order their products.

Another example of FOMO marketing is to display the number of consumers who are viewing the same product which the consumer is considering in an online or mobile shopping platform. This helps in bringing to the consumers' notice that the product is in demand and they may miss out on the deal if the stocks are limited. Both social proof and scarcity principles are at play here.

» CHAPTER 5 «

Marketing to Millennials

Millennials are the cornerstone of today's consumerism. Presently, Millennials have a more substantial economic influence than any other generation alive. Due to their peculiar tastes and preferences, Millennials force marketers and businesses to find innovative and original ideas for reaching out to them.

As explained in the previous chapters, the Millennial generation came of age during a time of rapid technological change, globalisation and economic disruption hence Millennials tend to lean towards purpose-driven brands whose vision aligns with their thought process. They have easy access to a plethora of information at their fingertips, and they are willing to spend more on comfort and experiences rather than on materialistic items.

To keep up with the Millennial expectations, businesses not only require realigning their time-tested business models but may also need a more fundamental introspection on what they stand for and promote as brands.

A Marketer's Dilemma

Despite being criticised as superficial and materialistic, statistics point out that Millennials are more interested in experiences than in material goods. While they seek the best deals for mundane purchases from groceries to hair cuts, Millennials would not think twice before spending sizeable amounts on their CrossFit memberships.

Marketing to Millennials can be a rewarding or excruciating experience depending on whether you hit the "right notes". A good product or an experience can literally "sell itself" if made viral by a delighted customer who can share and "hashtag" all the good things about their expericnces. Yet a few disgruntled customers can be highly vocal and cause severe damage to the brand bandwagon.

Huge businesses and business models have traditionally relied upon creating a distinctive brand with a dedicated following, thus ensuring a constant stream of revenue from these brand loyalists. However, Millennials seem to have a strange dichotomy in the way they perceive and treat brands. While traditional brands focused on brand identity and uniformity, Millennials tend to see brands as dynamic personas with their distinct characteristics and flaws. Actions of brands, brand ambassadors and their promoters are viewed critically in terms of issues that Millennials care about and large swings in brand equity can be observed overnight if some of these changes perceptually.

Most of us would remember Gillette dropping Tiger Woods as their brand ambassador following a series of tumultuous scandals involving the superstar golfer. Brands no longer want to associate themselves with celebrities or issues which can adversely impact their brand image.

The Millennial Mantra

On July 5, 2016, Nintendo's share price closed at 14,490 Yen (JPY) at the Tokyo Stock Exchange, having been around the same range for the entire calendar year. Yet, by July 19th it had scaled to a high of 31,770 Yen, a staggering growth of 119%. This Super Mario-esque run was fuelled by the launch of *Pokémon Go*, an augmented reality mobile game which went on to become an instant classic. It took just 20 days to gross USD 100 Million in revenue from the day of its launch. According to Guinness World Records, *Pokémon Go* made the record for the most revenue grossed by a mobile game in its first month, generating over USD 200 million. It also became the top-grossing mobile game app in 55 different countries simultaneously. It went on the become the world's most downloaded mobile game in its first month, topping the mobile download charts in 70 different countries.

The runaway success of *Pokémon Go* can be majorly accredited to its acceptance by the Millennial generation who instantly fell in love with a potent concoction of childhood nostalgia and cutting-edge technology. With a negligible marketing budget, the game sold itself through millions of user-generated hashtags and shares on social media along with excited users sharing locations of "PokéStops" and "Pokémon Gyms" in real-time.

The *Pokémon Go* example illustrates how brands can successfully target the Millennial mind using a common set of techniques, which marketers need to learn and perfect while dealing with Millennials as customers.

Following are the three Mantras for reaching out to and capturing the Millennial mindshare:

- Storytelling
- Relatability and relevance
- Enablement through technology

Putting the Mantras Into Action

1. **Social media presence:** It goes without saying, one needs to be where one's customer is. As seen in previous chapters, Millennials tend to communicate, shop, engage, and bond over social media. As a result, screen time and social media usage is consistently growing in quantity and scope. An engaging social media presence is hence indispensable for brands to connect with their target audience.

2. **Content for social media:** With more and more brands thronging to social media, it becomes imperative for their content to be compelling to break the clutter. Brands today need to create marketing personas on their social media which are relevant to its consumers and the products. A standard brand message across varied platforms is critical to convey the brand essence to the consumers using a voice and tone, which is relatable and authentic.

3. **Engaging audiences:** Unlike brands in the era of print and TV advertising, today's brands need to be visible on social media, engaging with consumers in new and innovative ways. A viral post or relatable meme can generate millions of views, retweets, shares, thereby giving free publicity and authenticity to the brand message. Brands must increase engagement by urging users to post pictures, comments, videos and stories to their channels tagging their social media handles and with appropriate hashtags.

4. **Creating social proof:** Restaurant and food chains offer instant discounts to customers who check-in at their outlet, posting images or content using advertised hashtags. Partnering with celebrities and domain-specific influencers help brands reach out to targeted social media audiences and showcase product quality and performance.

5. **Building brands with a purpose:** Millennial consumers aspire to a lifestyle that is authentic and purpose-driven. They also feel it is essential, that brands engaging with them display the same purpose and vision to "make the world a better place". A conscious effort is being made by the brands today to enhance its image by aligning themselves with global and topical issues such as environmental protection, gender and racial issues, education or health. This

helps them to catch the attention of the prospective buyers and helps engage with them across various media platforms.

6. **Nothing but the truth:** Having grown up in the midst of multiple coupons, lotteries and flash sales, Millennials display a profound scepticism towards anything that intends to sell or promote a product or service, whether directly or garbed as infomercials or advertorials. Misleading or exaggerated claims regarding performance or pricing may do more harm than benefit while dealing with this generation. All advertising must therefore be frank, fair and forthcoming.

7. **Do Not Sell Products, Sell Experiences:** With the growth in the tertiary economy and focus on experiential selling, every product today has a service component. In contrast, the delivery of every service is inevitably linked to one or more products. This phenomenon is reflected in the buying behaviour of Millennials as well, who yearn for memorable experiences and quality of service. Today, Millennials are purchasing for the experiences they get from the products and services they buy. Brands will tend to lose out in the medium and long run if they focus primarily on getting the purchase transaction done

without having planned on post-purchase service and engagement.

8. **Value is King:** We have already established that Millennials are acutely conscious of the value proposition offered by a product or service and would avoid spending beyond its perceived value. Each brand thus needs to articulate, communicate and deliver a clear value proposition keeping in mind the habits and aspirations of this segment. The key is to offer great value at a reasonable price while ensuring the product does not appear cheap in the eyes of the consumer.

9. **Story Selling:** Everyone likes a good story and Millennials are no different. The product or services offered, and the brand itself needs to create and tell engaging stories. These stories need to be communicated to audiences through social media posts and blogs. Even better, brands should give consumers something to share and talk about with their friends and peers. H&M managed to create positive word of mouth and PR through its "Be a fashion recycler" campaign where users could donate old garments and also get a 15% discount voucher for each medium-sized bag donated. In the era of UGC (User Generated Content), brands not only need to tell stories but also create storyboards to engage with consumers and let them be a part of the story itself.

Screenshot Courtesy: HM.com

10. **Hear them out:** As compared to previous generations, Millennials are more vocal and assertive when it comes to dealing with the brands they purchase. Their experience and affinity with a brand largely depend upon the responsiveness, and transparency exhibited by the brand while communicating with them, whether through media outlets or customer service touchpoints. Listening to their customers has been the mantra for hugely successful brands.

In 2009, Domino's Pizza deliveries were down 6% over the previous year. In the same year, they finished last in the Brand Keys[1] taste preference survey in the USA. On analysis, they realised that their menu and recipes were more than 50 years old and needed a changeover. So they encouraged consumers to try out their newer pizzas and invited feedback directly from consumers using social media platforms like Facebook, YouTube, Twitter leveraging hashtag #newpizza to improve their brand and of course the pizza based on direct customer feedback. The results were phenomenal - their next Q1 results saw a 14% increase in revenue. Consequently, by the end of 2010, the company's share price went up by 130%.

11. **Influencer Marketing**: When compared with traditional advertising, Millennials tend to rely more on authentic and relatable sources of product information such as expert reviews, tutorials, test drive and unboxing videos. Online platforms such as Instagram, YouTube and blogs offer videos and write-ups curated and created by independent creators and contributors popularly referred to as influencers. These "non-celebrity celebrities" may have social media followers running into millions, and can make or break a brand.

Influencers are subject matter experts who cater to an engaged and relatively homogenous audience. Their views are considered more authentic and trustworthy, causing ripples of responses among their followers. Kylie Jenner, the social media sensation (181 million followers on Instagram and 25 million on Twitter) caused a USD 1.5 Billion loss in Snap Inc's market capitalisation with just one tweet in 2018 – "sooo does anyone else not open Snapchat anymore? Or is it just me... ugh this is so sad."

Image/ Post Credit: Twitter/ @KylieJenner

Given the power wielded by influencers today, brands must choose the right fitment of influencers to promote their products and services to relevant audiences in the desired tone and imagery.

12. **Leveraging FOMO:** As we have explained in the opening chapters, Millennials are more prone to

experiencing FOMO than others. Thus, brands would be well advised to leverage this phenomenon to reach out to the Millennials. A cohesive strategy around marketing using FOMO will not only help marketers to break the clutter but also save valuable marketing rupees or dollars, and be closer to this demography.

The next part of this book deals with actionable approaches, case studies and practical insights on how to leverage Fear of Missing Out as a marketing tool.

» CHAPTER 6 «

Crafting FOMO in Marketing Strategy

With the ushering in of an age dominated by digital media, high-speed internet access and increased reliance on the internet for day to day needs, no brand or product can afford to ignore an effective social media strategy. Unlike in the past decades, where having an impressive website and social media following was considered a desirable yet dispensable feature, the coming decade will propel digital marketing to the status of a survival skill. Marketers who understand the dynamics of digital marketing and utilise its full potential shall invariably fare much better as compared to their counterparts who are content with participating in the same as a side hustle.

Tools like SEO, SEM, keyword marketing, social media marketing, content marketing, email marketing may be the building blocks of digital marketing. Still, without a thorough understanding of factors driving the behaviour of their audiences, these tools may prove to be way less than adequate. Emerging technologies such as AI/ ML, Big Data and cloud marketing will undoubtedly change the face of marketing in the 2020s. Yet, socio-cultural phenomena shaping consumer behaviour will provide the direction of efforts and innovation. Major social trends such as feminism, environmental activism and LGBTQ movement have made their presence felt not only in the political and social arenas but also given rise to trends and practices within marketing and advertising. FOMO appears to be a potent phenomenon for marketers to use while crafting their marketing strategies.

As demonstrated in the earlier chapters, the Fear of Missing Out has evolved to embrace various facets of modern life. It can be utilised as a versatile tool in the marketer's quiver. Modern-day marketers now have the tools, techniques and the platforms to craft this fear into a perception of urgency and exclusivity for the younger generation, thereby making promotional campaigns more engaging and effective. A well-crafted marketing strategy leveraging FOMO will not only deliver higher visibility and recall; it can be a sure-shot way of getting multi-fold ROI on marketing spends.

A Marketer's Guide to Leveraging FOMO

Creating Urgency

The purpose of most marketing efforts is to either induce purchase behaviour or hasten the purchase cycle. The idea of generating a sense of urgency in the consumer's mind is a time-tested technique and works brilliantly and even more so in the age of digital media.

The modern man lives with a multitude of deadlines. There is no method, more certain, of getting a response from anyone as compared to announcing an impending deadline. Consumers are more likely to end up making that impulsive purchase when a clock is ticking than when they might have had a chance to think more about completing the purchase in detail.

Black Friday Sale, Cyber Monday, Flipkart Big Billion Days or Amazon Great Indian Sale are all examples of these techniques of creating urgency. All have the same philosophy – offering the audiences deals they cannot miss with a discount on them and limiting it to a short duration, 24 hours to a couple of days at max.

> *Creating limited stock offers will help trigger consumer's FOMO who would be consistently tempted to act and make a purchase before the clock stops ticking.*

Let us evaluate four of the strategies which are consistently successful in creating a sense of urgency.

Flash Sales

The most common form of FOMO marketing is Flash sales. Flash sales intend to create urgency of purchase due to limited stock availability or a limited timeframe for which a deal is available. It gives the consumer a sense of scarcity and helps shorten the purchase cycle. It happens to be widely used by both online as well as offline retailers. Amazon Lighting Deals or Limited-Edition cosmetic collections by Kylie Jenner both use this tactic to ensure faster stock uptake, triggering FOMO by announcing limited availability or exclusivity.

> *Brands can thus ensure higher recall and quicker stock liquidation by launching products with a limited period or limited-edition options.*

Display Stock Level

Nothing triggers a palpable sense of scarcity as much as a ticker announcing just how many items of the desired product remain in stock. When the product consumer has been eyeing is highlighted as being in short supply, the pressure to buy the product elevates to the next level. By displaying the count of items available for purchase, marketers are urging the consumers to make a purchase decision since it is 'now or never'.

Limiting the number of seats available for a particular event and showcasing the availability can work wonders for an event or a service like online courses or classrooms. Online travel websites and apps such as Redbus.in use this technique when they display the number of seats available on a route, thereby, giving a clear warning to the customer of the possibility of not being able to make the purchase 'in time'.

A classic example of limited stock availability is witnessed in ticketing queues for Wimbledon. A limited number of wristbands are issued only to those who are in front of the queue. The number of wristbands issued matches the number of tickets available for each court on that day. Each wristband has a detachable "court" tally which needs to be handed over to the cashier for issuing a corresponding ticket.

> ***Stock levels for sought after products can thus be displayed to customers to sustain their interest and ensure purchase decisions are not delayed or postponed.***

Pre-Order

Almost everyone prefers to enjoy enviable experiences before others. Marketers have been using this insight for years, launching myriad early bird offers and exclusive previews to lure their customers. The same proposition can be made more alluring by adding a tangible advantage, such as a special price or additional benefit for the given price.

Apple has leveraged the pre-order strategy for astounding results. The delivery timelines for iPhone X in the year 2017 went from less than a week to more than a month within 30 minutes of opening up for pre-order. "Call of Duty: Modern Warfare", a First-Person Shooter video game launched in the year 2019 brought in USD 600 million in revenue in its first three days of launch and also became the most digitally pre-ordered game on PS4 ever.

> *With the advent of online ordering and e-commerce, pre-order will become more vital as a tool for generating pre-release buzz and scoring quick numbers at the time of launch. Marketers can significantly benefit from triggering FOMO by successfully leveraging the pre-order tactic.*

Highlight Missed Opportunities

Picture this: you just filled up your cart with groceries for a full month. As you advance to checkout and pay on your app, a popup message appears on the app. The message tries to lure you into purchasing the 'premium service' which would substantially reduce your delivery cost and help you avail discounts on your purchases. Additionally, the 'premium service' is priced at a similar amount that you would have spent had you not availed their offer. Would you still checkout without opting for the service promoted?

Travel website Booking.com uses another technique to their advantage by showcasing inventory that just got sold out. It displays the list of hotels which have run out of rooms on the dates you were planning to book on with a very appropriate and a direct FOMO inducing heading - "You missed it!".

> ***Another way of using FOMO in a marketing strategy is by highlighting opportunities that customers recently missed. When consumers realise they have lost a good deal because they could not make a decision quickly, FOMO will kick in compelling them to make a decision soon on the next product or service, lest it also slips away.***

Social Proof

Social proof is a handy FOMO-inducing-marketing tool at the marketers' disposal. We have already detailed out the benefits of social proof in the earlier chapter.

Social proof boosts the consumers' FOMO by emphasising on the brand or products' popularity. Reviews and testimonials about a brand or a product on social media from existing customers go a long way in creating the required level of trust in prospective buyers. When customers get to read the positive experiences about the product from other individuals, they start feeling more comfortable with the brand and become more inclined to make a purchase themselves.

Sometimes, social proof is all that customers, especially Millennials, need to decide on a purchase.

The following techniques, when incorporated in a marketing strategy, help generate substantial social proof.

Display What Others Are Purchasing or Viewing

Nothing kindles the competitive spirit more than a comparison with the activities of the fellow human beings. FOMO can be induced by arousing this competitive spirit amongst fellow human beings which is based on comparison and competition. Displaying what other consumers are ordering or adding in their online carts triggers FOMO while also disclosing how popular their chosen items are.

__Letting consumers know that others are also interested in the same product at the exact moment provides a strong motivation for the consumers to proceed with their buying decision.__

While this generates sufficient social proof that many people are interested in your product, it also makes the consumers feel that they are competing with others to buy the same product. This kindling of competitive spirit helps drive them to make that purchase spontaneously.

Zulily.com, an American e-commerce company, generates FOMO by showcasing the number of people currently viewing an item and the quantity sold recently. Marketers can employ such techniques to improve conversions and minimise cart abandonment (abandoning a virtual shopping cart before completing the payment process).

Screenshot Courtesy: Zulily.com

Ratings and Reviews

Millennials are more likely to read reviews before deciding upon a purchase. Online reviews and ratings go a long way in generating the necessary social proof for a brand. A Millennial customer is likely to cancel their purchase if they come across many negative reviews. The same is true for online ratings as well. A product below a benchmark rating (example 3 star on a 5-point scale) is much less likely to be purchased as compared to another product with a higher rating even with a reasonable price differential.

While ratings quantify the quality and performance of a product, reviews from customer's real-life experience are perceived to be more authentic and relatable. Use of relevant keywords by reviewers while sharing their experience can help potential buyers to determine whether this is the product they want.

> *Businesses must, therefore, not only focus on getting good ratings but also encourage and incentivise their customers to add reviews based on their usage of the product.*

To provide an additional layer of authenticity to the rating process, businesses can add a tag stating "Verified Purchase" alongside the product review submitted. Better ratings and use of relevant keywords in reviews can help generate the required FOMO to push the customer towards a purchase decision.

Swiggy, a popular Indian food delivery startup, has made effective use of the rating system. They have linked the incentives of their delivery partners with ratings given by the customers on their delivery experience whereas, food quality and packaging are rated independently for the restaurants. This methodology not only enhances customer experience but also motivates its delivery partners.

Screenshot Courtesy: Amazon.in

User-Generated Content – #Hashtag Marketing

Hashtags are an easy way to track customer engagement with a brand or a campaign. By using hashtags on social media posts and encouraging followers to do the same, brands can create necessary buzz around either the product or the service, or even the brand campaign with a unified message or story.

Creating a campaign encouraging users to submit their images or videos in combination with a given hashtag or tagging the brand's social media handle draws in the consumers through social proof. Rather than being mere recipients of a brand story, consumers feel part of the brand's journey, actively creating and adding meaning to the campaign's storyboard.

In the recent past, brands, as well as different movements, have gained popularity and momentum by running successful hashtag campaigns. Socio-cultural and activist movements have also garnered broad level support through hashtags such as #MeToo, #FridaysforFuture, #OccupyWallStreet and #BlackLivesMatter.

> ***While brands would desire to ride on the hashtag bandwagon, it is vital for the campaign to be authentic and relevant to create genuine interest among masses. Finding a suitable topic and creating a memorable hashtag holds the key to a successful marketing campaign generating substantial social proof.***

Image Credit: Instagram/ @fridaysforfuture.europe

Customer Testimonials

Relevance and reliability of a product or service can often be more important in a purchase decision rather than features and capabilities alone, especially in a B2B (Business-to-Business) scenario. By adding testimonials of their clients which state the benefits attained by using the seller's product or service, brands can successfully foster a favourable mindset amongst prospective customers.

Popular video-conferencing service, Zoom has a dedicated section on its website showcasing positive customer testimonials highlighting features that they found most useful.

Similar testimonials can be added to the landing page and social media handles to ensure a positive perception among prospective clients.

Screenshot Courtesy: Zoom.us

Influencer Marketing

As we have already mentioned, customers, especially Millennials, trust opinions from seemingly authentic sources more than traditional advertisements from brands themselves. Therefore, it makes sense for today's marketers to generate favourable opinions from sources who offer expertise and authenticity on the product or service category.

This is where the growing role of influencers comes in. An influencer can be a celebrity or an industry expert with a very active and dedicated social media following. When someone of that stature talks about a brand, it can provide significant impetus to a marketing campaign.

Partnering with social media influencers and 'micro-influencers' is a direct way to reach out to customers while also kindling the Fear of Missing Out in them.

Forbes or Autocar magazines were previously seen as authentic sources while evaluating the purchase of premium luxury cars. Whereas, influencers like Alex Hirschi (aka Supercar Blondie with more than 30 million followers on various social media channels) have now emerged as substantially more reliable and approachable sources for the decision making. Their views and opinions can prove to be decisive for the success or failure of brands operating within their domain.

Screenshot Courtesy: SupercarBlondie.com

As Featured on…

If a brand or product has featured in reputable media publications, it is essential to let customers know that. Even highlighting media publications in the form of its logo on the brand's website or app is enough to build credibility around a product or a brand.

> ***Brands can further substantiate through a reference or quote from the publication. Getting featured in a reputable media source adds credibility to the brand.***

Authors, Photographers, Startups, Freelancers and Small Businesses can use this technique to build up trust amongst their audiences. Prasenjeet Yadav, an India based National Geographic Explorer, uses his website (www.prasenjeetyadav.com) to showcase awards and publications featuring him to build credibility around his work.

PUBLICATIONS

- NPR
- The Wire
- Wired.in
- Scroll.in : Science photography Initiative
- ShootForScience : A science photography Workshop
- Photo Exhibition : Telluride Mountain Film festival
- National Geographic Traveller India (2015)
- National Geographic Your Shot : Urban Wildlife - Final Story
- The Phoblographer
- Storytelling
- Scroll.in (2015)
- Scientific American (2015)
- Saevus (2015)
- Conservation India (2015)
- Conservation Biology (2014)
- Science Daily (2014)
- Stanford Journal (News) (2014)
- Better Photography (2014)
- Nature India (2014)
- Asia Times (2014)
- Saevus (2013)
- Indian Express (2013)
- Conservation Genetics Resources (2012)
- Sanctuary Asia (2011)
- Bhraman (2010)

AWARDS

- National Geographic Nature photographer of the year : Landscape category
- Recipient of the Team Gilka Award at Missouri photojournalism workshop - 68
- Recipient of McDougall Overall Excellence in Editing Scholarship to attend MPW68
- INK Fellow 2016
- Banff Mountain film photo essay - Winner 2016
- National Geographic Conservation Trust Grant (2015)
- National Geographic Young Explorers (2014)
- Rufford Small Grant for Conservation (2014)
- Nature India: Science Photographer of the Year : 2nd Prize (2014)
- Shrushti : Wildlife photographer of the Year (2014)
- Saevus India : Pixel Perfect : (2013)
- Winner : Nature Trailblazers : India's only assignment photography contest (2013,2014)
- Sanctuary : Wildlife Photographer of the year (Special Mention) (2011)

Screenshot Courtesy: PrasenjeetYadav.com

Awards, Certifications and Memberships

Customers prefer to purchase from companies and brands they can trust. Awards and technical certifications go a long way in establishing this trust. There are various accrediting bodies like ISO, BIS, PMP which issue certificates pertaining to process, skill or product quality. These can be further showcased to communicate reliable performance to prospective customers. Both individual professionals and businesses benefit from such certifications. Constantly updating recent awards, recognitions, and certifications keep the brand's followers on social media engaged.

Having a blue tick-mark against the brand's social handle also adds credibility and encourages prospective customers to follow brands and stay connected. The social platform, in this case, recognizes the brand as famous and influential enough to be awarded the tick-mark.

The Times Food and Nightlife Awards recognize and reward the best in the hospitality industry, and their certifications are proudly displayed by the winning as well as nominated brands. Online payment gateways such as Razorpay display their ISO 27001 compliance status to assure their clients of the highest levels of information security.

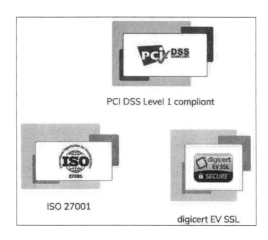

Screenshot Courtesy: Razorpay.com

All businesses, whether big or small, technical or artistic, must display awards and certifications earned to stand apart from the crowd and generate social proof.

Referrals

Referral marketing, put simply, banks upon current customers to introduce brands and products to prospective customers within their social circle. Like other forms of social proof, this works because people trust a recommendation when someone they trust endorses it. Moreover, someone referring a product to their friends and family implies that they have had a good experience with it.

To increase the chances of customers recommending a product or service, brands often add a reward or an incentive when people sign up or purchase based on referrals from an existing customer. These incentives may be offered to the referrer, the referee, or both in the form of a freebie or a discount.

Dropbox utilizes the referral technique in getting customers to sign up for their cloud storage services by giving free extra storage space to both the existing and the new customers being referred.

> *Businesses would benefit from offering moderate referral incentives based on current business objectives, whether acquiring new customers or enhancing usage and loyalty among existing ones.*

Numbers Matter

As humans are social animals, nothing justifies a behaviour more than a large number of fellow human beings doing the same. Subscriber or consumer base count is thus an important indicator of social proof and can build credibility among potential customers.

> *Showcasing how many visitors a website gets, how many downloads or installs an app has had till date or how many views/ retweets/ upvotes/ likes a social media post has, are all techniques to generate social proof. Numbers help reinforce the broad appeal and hence superiority of a product or service.*

WordPress, an online website creation platform, claims that "38% of the web" is built on their platform. With this statistic, people are more likely to choose WordPress for developing their website as against other similar platforms.

> # Welcome to the world's most popular website builder.
>
> 38% of the web is built on WordPress. More bloggers, small businesses, and Fortune 500 companies use WordPress than all other options combined. Join the millions of people that call WordPress.com home.
>
> Start your website

Screenshot Courtesy: WordPress.com

Foster Exclusivity

One of the most successful types of marketing relies on creating a sense of exclusiveness triggering a feeling of importance among the "in-group". Still better, this exclusiveness often comes coupled with special access rights or priority privileges for the group members. For those who could not join the "in-group", being left out is bound to create a sense of FOMO.

Creating an exclusive club with special privileges makes the "in-group" feel special and rewarded while leaving others envious. Another way of triggering FOMO through exclusivity is by offering limited-edition exclusive variants of sought-after products or services.

Amazon Prime Membership is an apt example of fostering exclusivity. Through a paid subscription model, Amazon Prime members get exclusive offers which include free and fast shipping; exclusive movies and television shows through Prime Video; ad-free and downloadable music through Prime Music; access to hundreds of eBooks; and exclusive early access to deals and discounts, be it on daily lightning deals or whenever a sale festival is on.

> *Brands and businesses can create enrolment programmes and attach attractive pricing or privilege access with them, encouraging non-members to seek out enrolment. Alternatively, limited edition variants of products and services, either through a limited count or for a limited period can be launched and positioned in a way that only a select few can get their hands on.*

Loss Aversion

As discussed in Chapter 4, loss aversion is another characteristic of consumer behaviour closely linked with FOMO. Research has shown that the psychological pain of losing something is nearly twice as powerful as the pleasure of gaining something of the same value. In order words, humans are psychologically geared to react impulsively in situations where a loss is envisioned, as compared to when a gain is expected.

Loss aversion, when used as a FOMO marketing technique, can effectively generate higher conversions for a sales or marketing campaign. Following are some essential tactics to include the loss aversion technique in marketing campaigns to substantially improve sales conversions.

Reward Programmes

Reward programmes are a loss aversion technique for brands to develop customer loyalty. While giving them exclusive benefits, it encourages them to become repeat customers. Reward or loyalty programmes offer customers additional value like discounts, freebies or exclusive access to new product line ups or early access for an upcoming sale.

The lure of exclusive rewards urges customers to develop a long-term relationship with a brand, resulting in higher lifetime value and sustained purchase frequency. American Express (Amex) has developed a strong loyalty amongst its customers using its Membership Rewards (MR) programme for its credit and charge cards. Under this programme, Amex cardholders accumulate "loyalty points" for purchases, referrals and through limited-time "point multiplier" offers. Each card category offers special privileges such as free access to airport lounges and differential redemption rates, often linked with points thresholds or "targets" to be achieved within a financial period. By linking consumer purchases with thresholds offering special rewards, Amex is able to ensure customer loyalty as well as sustained usage.

> *When planning to execute a loss aversion strategy through reward programmes, it is crucial for brands to ensure regular and continued communication with their members of the reward programmes. Loss aversion can be triggered by adding an expiry date to accumulated points; and further, displaying the required points to reach the next level of reward threshold.*

Free Trial Offers

Endowment effect refers to how humans tend to prefer objects they already possess over those they do not.[1] The term 'endowment effect' was coined in the year 1980 by U.S. economist Richard Thaler. Marketers' use this concept in free trials to acquire new users or buyers. From the customer's viewpoint, receiving a trial offer can do two things – it showcases the features and the relevance of the product to the prospective buyers, while at the same time it generates a sense of ownership towards the product or service, thus triggering the endowment effect.

At the end of a trial offer, in case the customer intends to continue the benefits of the product or service, he is required to either buy at the market price or pay a subscription fee. Endowment effect forces them to perceive a loss of continued benefits as higher than the price to be paid, often turning the beneficiaries of free trial into paid consumers.

Norton Antivirus offers a free trial of Norton Family, a cloud-based parental control service for a period of six months. At the end of the free period, customers need to subscribe to a paid version equivalent or higher to the version enjoyed during the free trial.

> *Brands should not just offer a free trial to their customers for a substantial duration to build perceived ownership of the product or service, but they should also regularly engage with the customers during the free trial period highlighting the benefits and advantages of subscription as well as triggering FOMO by reminding them of the limited duration for which the trial is available.*

Discount Codes/Coupons

Yet another application of the endowment effect is discount codes or coupons. They utilise the loss aversion mindset to initiate new purchases or repurchase amongst existing users.

Coupons and vouchers trigger loss aversion behaviour more vigorously as compared to other forms of sales promotion. Customers feel a sense of ownership with an exclusive or time-limited coupon and experience an urgency to make a purchase, being goaded into taking action by FOMO.

Zomato, a food delivery platform uses contextual coupons to boost sales by offering limited period discount codes. These codes are promoted through multi-modal advertising campaigns, e.g. the coupon "MAXSAFETY" was used to highlight the steps being taken during COVID-19 pandemic.

While offering discount coupons and codes, marketers should ensure an appropriate redemption period and value so that customers feel a sense of urgency in using the coupons and also develop a positive image of the brand. The code used can also be chosen to highlight a special occasion or campaign like a festival, special event or a cause.

Package Deals/Bundle Pricing

Bundling is a practical example of second-degree price discrimination. Product packages or bundles are put together for upselling across industries and sector. While in most cases these products are available for purchase separately, buying a 'bundle' often results in savings in cost and effort. The 'bundle' is usually priced lower than the individual price of each item to highlight the savings enjoyed by the customer on the bundled purchase. "Combo Meals" at a fast-food restaurant is a perfect example of bundle pricing wherein for a single price, an entrée (main dish), a drink and a side dish is offered to the customer. With their popular bundled offer, the Happy Meal, McDonald's has generated billions of dollars in sales. Further, they have even become the world's largest distributor of toys since every Happy Meal box comes with a toy.

Image Courtesy: McDonald's India blog/ https://mcdonaldsblog.in

For brands planning to offer bundles of products or services, it is worthwhile to carefully identify the right products to bundle and ensure that customer

value is built and communicated clearly to maximise adoption. Brands can bundle slow-moving products with high moving ones to drive sales or bundle complementary products and services to augment ticket size.

At the very core, FOMO attempts to appeal to consumers by triggering emotions and instincts linked with the behaviour of humans as social beings. Any marketing strategy can be refined and amplified by adding one or more components of FOMO. Marketers can craft an endless variety of engaging and goal-oriented campaigns through the creative use of tools discussed here.

» CHAPTER 7 «

Case Studies
The Binge Trap – Netflix

The Netflix Story

Netflix's marketing strategy is a lesson for all marketers and not just for those from the entertainment industry. Netflix has become a synonym for online streaming not only for its unparalleled movie library or the Originals it produces but also for the remarkable marketing campaigns it employs to promote its new content.

Having a deep understanding of their audience's demographics, Netflix smartly leverages this information while crafting its acquisition and engagement strategy. Since its users are typically tech-savvy, FOMO plays a vital role in its marketing campaigns. Netflix has hooked millions of Millennials on to its platform, a majority even cutting the cord from cable television, replacing it with online streaming.

According to a 2019 survey by HowToWatch, the average amount of time Millennials would spend watching Netflix is roughly equal to 13 years of their lives.[1] In their study, the average Millennial Netflix viewer responded by saying that they watched 6.6 hours of Netflix a day, which works out to be about 46.2 hours a week or almost two days in a week.

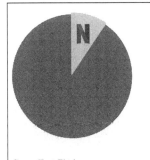

Millennials will spend over 16% of their expected life span watching Netflix.

Source: *HowtoWatch*

The platform has been steadily growing its repository of movies and series. Not just of various third-party production houses, Netflix is also ramping up its Original content titles which includes series like *House of Cards, The Crown, Stranger Things, Orange Is the New Black,*

Sacred Games and *Delhi Crime*. Several Netflix offerings have won accolades at significant award events like Golden Globe, Emmys and Oscars.

Netflix has witnessed remarkable growth from its initial days as a DVD rental service relying on postal mail. Started in 1997 by Reed Hastings and Marc Rudolph for online movie rentals, Netflix has grown to a behemoth 182 million subscribers clocking $20.2 billion in revenue in the year 2019.[2] Such stupendous growth has resulted from an adaptive business model, frequently evolving to outpace the competition and leaving their customers delighted.

The first change came in 1999 when Netflix ditched their "pay for rental" model for a subscription-based model. Under the rental model, users would browse and order movie DVDs they required on the Netflix website, and Netflix would post them to their homes. After renters had finished with the DVDs, they would simply post them back to Netflix. Users paid DVD rental charges plus postage charges.

Under the new subscription model, Netflix allowed subscribers to keep rented DVDs for as long as they wanted, but they had to return the previous one if they wanted to rent out another DVD. The subscription model was an innovative approach to pricing. This model provided respite to the customers from the late fees, which was priced at USD 40 by DVD rental companies at that time. Notably, Blockbuster, Netflix's bigger rival, earned USD 800 million in late fees alone in the year 2000.

By the year 2010, Netflix was at it again, changing its business model to introduce a streaming service, a popular and familiar model, currently. Netflix's streaming service changed the way people watched movies, eventually forcing laggards like Blockbuster to shut shop.

Even a decade later despite stiff competition from big rivals such as Amazon Prime, Disney and Apple joining the fray, Netflix remains the preferred streaming entertainment service provider with nearly half the industry's subscriber base in the quarter ending March 2020.

Binge Watching as a Business Model

In the 21st century, customers are used to having whatever they want - as soon as they want it. The same applies to entertainment as well. Gone are the days of waiting for the next episode of your favourite show; customers want to watch the whole series in one go. This practice of watching multiple episodes of a television show in a single sitting even has a name - Binge-watching.

According to an analysis from Omdia Channels & Programming Intelligence, Netflix launched 657 first-run original titles in 2019, compared to 386 in 2018, which accelerated the frenzy of binge-watching.[2] This launch considerably increased the running time of its Originals from 1,537 hours in 2018 to 2,769 hours in 2019, recording a growth of 80% in the given year. Its nearest competitor Amazon Prime added considerably lower numbers of new titles, clocking 314 hours of viewing with 70 original programmes.

In the year 2019, a whopping 58% of Netflix's original content was produced outside of the USA. Hence, it has been noticed that binge-watching fever has gripped countries and societies across the globe like never before.

Unlike traditional television series which typically release a new episode every week, Netflix releases all episodes of its series at once.

This method of releasing all episodes at once has also altered viewers' viewing habits. Whether they are commuting to and from work or relaxing in the comfort of their homes, users can watch the latest television series for hours at a time. Instead of waiting weeks and in some cases several months to disclose the cliff-hangers, subscribers can plunge deeply into the Netflix universe of streaming and enjoy the unravelling in one go.

With the amount of exciting content Netflix is putting up on its platform year after year, it raises the curiosity level in its audience, stimulating them to consume its coveted content as quickly as possible and race forward to the next episode.

Fear of Missing Out (FOMO) is one of the driving forces behind the binge-watching phenomenon. Since Millennials and Generation Z form a large part of the audience, anything that is watched is bound to be flaunted on social media. Even when a user has not watched the latest season of say *Stranger Things*, their peers would have. They would inevitably discuss its nuances and twists on social media, triggering bouts of FOMO.

Not only missing episodes but even being left behind on the series trail can also leave the viewer vulnerable to FOMO. The fear of being left behind in any conversation related to the latest popular series is dreadful for the Millennial, and the only pre-emptive measure is to watch them all before anybody else would.

Yet, peer pressure is not the only force driving binge-watching behaviour. It takes a compelling social media buzz created through an ingenious media strategy to achieve sublime levels of viewer engagement.

Netflix's social media presence goes a lot beyond just being a pure marketing channel handle for announcing new launches. Their social media approach is about engaging audiences with frequent interactions infused with a dash of wit and humour. Netflix has mastered the art and science of reaching out to its viewers through innovative formats such as GIFs, memes, polls, and even questions posed to initiate engaging conversations about their content.

Netflix also makes the most of influencer marketing with top celebrities joining their social bandwagon to promote their newly launched content helping them further amplify its reach and awareness.

In the case of *Narcos*, a Netflix original, chronicling the life of Columbian drug lord Pablo Escobar, social media was used to generate oodles of excitement even before the series was launched. Much of the promotional content was not created around the plot, as it would have divulged the storyline and acted as a spoiler. Instead, Netflix launched the #Cokenomics campaign to promote the show through a series of fascinating infographics detailing the life and times of Pablo Escobar. For audiences across continents, who may or may not have heard of Escobar before, the hashtag helped in raising a much-needed hype triggering the Fear of Missing Out.

Through the life of the series, facts and figures about the economics of Colombian drug trade played a crucial role in sustaining viewers' attention. Contextual charts and infographics comparing the 'Medellin cartel' with popular cultural icons and even business corporations were shared and retweeted by viewers generating substantial social proof to drive engagement on social media platforms. These generally featured actual numbers from cocaine trade under Escobar to demonstrate the scale of operations during his era.

Image Credit: Instagram/ @Narcos

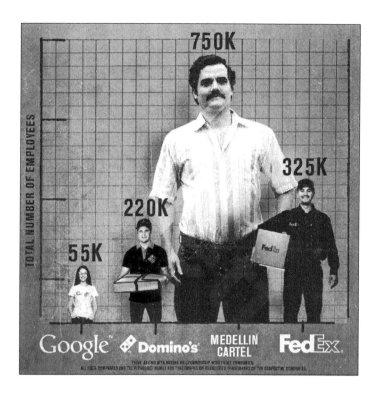

Image Credit: Instagram/ @Narcos

These tactics helped *Narcos* achieve the crowning glory of the most-mentioned Netflix original series on social media for 2015, clocking more than 100,000 social engagements (likes, comments, and shares) and helped establish the series as a cult-classic among Millennials.

With the iconic following, Netflix has garnered, social trends and memes inspired by its popular content have also emerged, purely generated and promoted by its fans on social media. The #BirdBoxChallenge was a social challenge generated entirely by fans of the Netflix thriller *Bird Box*. People across Facebook, Instagram and Twitter, shared videos of themselves completing everyday tasks blindfolded, recreating the struggle that the blindfolded lead star, Sandra Bullock, experiences in the movie with her two small children, 'Boy' and 'Girl' to survive.

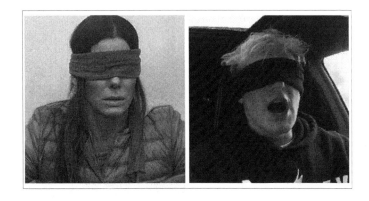

Photograph Courtesy: Netflix/ Sandra Bullock
(left) and YouTube/ Jake Paul (right)

The hashtag gained immense popularity giving *Bird Box* a record viewership of above 45 million in the first seven days of its release, as announced by Netflix themselves through their social media handles. Things got ridiculous as fans started to post more and more videos completing everyday tasks blindfolded, some of them getting injured in the process. Even Netflix had to step in, issuing a warning tweet cautioning viewers to exercise restraint and not get hurt while doing the #BirdBoxChallenge.

Image/ Post Credit: Twitter/ @netflix

For another one of its popular Originals, *Stranger Things*, which premiered in 2016, Netflix upped its social media campaign partnering with various brands and generating enough social proof to ensure sufficient FOMO in the Millennials. As the series was based in the 1980s, the promotional strategy leveraged the Millennials' nostalgia for the era in which they had grown up. By showcasing products and images from the period concerned, it helped the audience reconnect to childhood memories, translating into associations with the characters on screen.

Netflix tapped into this nostalgia with its social media campaign through a FOMO inducing mix of influencer marketing and social proof. Before the launch of the series, Netflix had partnered with Twitch, a popular live streaming platform for gamers, who hosted a four-hour live stream during which the influencers played video games in a 1980s themed basement resonating with the theme of the show. It offered an interactive experience where viewers voted on creepy things to create supernatural effects like flickering lights, flying books, and randomly shutting doors on the unsuspecting influencers who were busy playing the game. The broadcast ended with viewers being treated to an exclusive preview footage of the first episode.

For the launch of *Stranger Things Season 3*, Netflix partnered with around 75 different brands for in-episode brand placements while partnering brands also showcased products and campaigns linked with the series. The strategy turned out to be a win-win for both Netflix and the brands as it generated excitement and brand engagement across platforms through synchronised marketing efforts. While brands re-launched products and showcased *Stranger Things* themed items, *Stranger Things* promoted their products by carefully knitting them in the storyline itself.

The prominent brands that generated social proof for *Stranger Things* during the run-up of the show's launch were:

1. **Coca-Cola:** Coca Cola leveraged the Netflix partnership to relaunch its 1985's "New Coke" as a limited-edition product, producing 500,000 cans.

2. **Burger King:** Based on the storyline of *Stranger Things*, Burger King turned their most popular burger, The Whopper, upside down which was exclusively packaged with *Stranger Things* brand name and renamed it the 'Upside Down Whopper'. During the campaign period, they even rebranded themselves as 'Stranger King' while also styling their logo upside down.

3. **Nike:** Nike released a new 1980s inspired clothing line as part of the sports brand's collaboration with Netflix. In addition to the iconic sneaker models, the clothing collection also featured Hawkins High themed shirts, hoodies and sweatpants designed as if taken straight out of a scene from the show. Nike's collaboration appealed to fans' obsession with both 80's pop culture and the series, engaging the audiences and keeping the conversation going.

Post Credit: Instagram/ @CocaColaCo

Other notable brand partnerships include tie-ups with Microsoft and Baskin-Robbins. Microsoft launched Windows 1.0 inspired app that let users experience the interface which they had first released in the year 1985. Baskin-Robbins introduced unique *Stranger Things* themed flavours, and transformed few of their stores into a replica of 'Scoops Ahoy' store from the show's storyline.

Lego launched the *Stranger Things* collection set taking the show's popularity directly to Lego buyers. The playset featured a Lego replica of Will Byers' house, who is a leading protagonist in *Stranger Things*. Further, building upon the show's theme, the Lego set not only recreates the house in the real world, but when flipped, it reveals the Upside Down version of the house.

Netflix's Stranger Things Season Three released on July 4, 2019 and broke the Netflix record for its most-viewed series in the first four days of release.

By cleverly utilising FOMO in their campaigns, Netflix has proved through the success of its shows and their social media engagement levels, that the possibilities of brand engagement through FOMO inducing techniques are virtually limitless. Marketers need to accurately identify their target audiences and use these strategies through effective media campaigns to create immersive experiences that promote their brands or products while leveraging the art and science of generating FOMO.

Influencer Marketing Strategy – Daniel Wellington

With the explosive growth of social media platforms as the primary medium for connecting and gathering information, opportunities for promotion of brands and products using this medium have also grown manifold. This expansion has led to a simultaneous increase of influencers, who are popular social media users with a following which ranges from a few thousand to several million.

Influencers tend to keep their followers engaged by sharing interesting content and opinions, often asking their followers to retweet, share or vote in their polls to keep their channels interactive. They are often considered to be subject matter experts catering to a focused audience and seen as more authentic, relatable and trustworthy sources of information by their followers.

Realising their potential in promoting and forming opinions about brands and products, many marketers have roped in influencers to promote their brands. A mention or an announcement on their social media page can yield a significant boost to visibility and recall of the marketing campaign.

The rise of influencers on social media has opened enormous opportunities for brands looking to market their products and services to their target audience through social media "word of mouth". In many cases, micro-influencers (social media users with a limited number of followers generally between 1,000 to 100,000) are turning out to be more effective than celebrities for promoting different brands, products or services through social media endorsements.

Especially in the case of Millennial audiences, influencer marketing lets brands reach their target audience more reliably than traditional advertising, simultaneously generating the necessary social proof and triggering consumers' FOMO.

Daniel Wellington is an apt example of how to achieve brand success through influencer marketing. Founded in 2011 in Sweden by Filip Tysander, Daniel Wellington (abbreviated as DW), is a contemporary fashion brand that sells watches with minimalist designs. These watches come with interchangeable nylon straps, popularly known as NATO straps, which can be frequently swapped to change the look of the watch.

Daniel Wellington was one of the first few brands that understood the potential of influencer marketing and leveraged it for its success. Having started his business with an investment of just USD 15,000, the brand's founder, Tysander knew his marketing spends were limited and therefore decided to focus on social media marketing rather than go through the traditional advertising route.

Also cognizant of the fact that these peppy watches with their quirky straps would most certainly cater to the younger generation, he realised that the Millennials or Gen Y were his target audience. Since Millennials spend a considerable share of their time on social media, and Instagram is a very visual focused platform, choosing it as the primary marketing platform seemed to be the appropriate strategy.

Tysander realised that several micro-influencers on Instagram would generate more buzz and awareness for a Millennial-focused product than a few prominent celebrities or influencer endorsements. To execute this marketing strategy, he approached micro-influencers to create brand awareness about his watches.

Daniel Wellington offered free wristwatches to select few influencers who were willing to share pictures of the wristwatches on their Instagram account while using the hashtag #danielwellington. The influencers were also encouraged to create and share quirky content showcasing the watch and using the hashtag. Leveraging user-generated content (UGC) was a brilliant idea as it gave influencers complete liberty to shoot and showcase the watches in any way the influencers deemed fit. It gave influencers the artistic freedom to highlight the 'trendiness' of the product by assimilating their unique styles which are loved by their followers. It also made the #danielwellington campaign look more authentic as compared to any standardised advertising which is created through traditional advertising agencies.

Post Credit: Instagram/ @vaishnavi_andhale

To measure the reach of their campaign, Daniel Wellington gave the influencers unique discount coupons for giveaways to their followers along with the #danielwellington post. The discount coupons integrated multiple FOMO techniques in the campaign. Although the campaign kicked off using social proof through influencer marketing, the use of discount coupons triggered loss aversion by creating a sense of urgency in purchasing the watch at a discounted price.

Over time, the social media marketing campaign expanded with further FOMO-fuelled marketing opportunities. Daniel Wellington further widened the appeal of their campaign through more social proof, this time from their customers. Buyers of DW watches were encouraged to add user-generated content by sharing pictures sporting DW watches with #DWPickoftheDay hashtag to participate in "Pick of the Day" contest. Selected photo of the day shared on Instagram was awarded a new DW watch, and the winner got featured on DW's official Instagram page.

While winners of #DWPickoftheDay campaign got their moment under the sun, DW got immense publicity as the hashtag got mentioned in over 63 thousand posts. Initially, the hashtag #danielwellington was primarily promoted through influencers; it eventually gained momentum through consumers of the brand who participated in the contest and made the brand viral through their social media accounts. As of July 2020, #danielwellington has been used in over 2.3 million posts on Instagram alone.

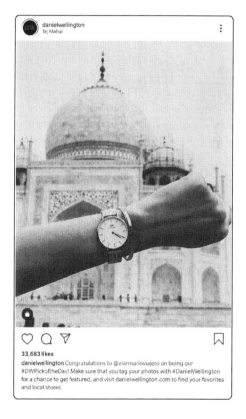

Post Credit: Instagram/ @danielwellington

According to a Socialbakers study, Daniel Wellington received the most influencer mentions for any brand on Instagram in 2018-19, receiving more than 20,000 mentions from 7,200 influencers.[1] DW's official Instagram account has reached more than 4.9 million followers, another key brand success indicator in the social media era.

Daniel Wellington's story demonstrates that harnessing the power of social media and effectively using FOMO to target and engage audiences can deliver manifold results as compared to traditional paid advertising. Especially in the case of smaller and upcoming brands, incorporating FOMO as a marketing strategy can help break the clutter and create an authentic brand following, resulting in higher recall and sales revenue.

Epilogue

As the battle to capture customer's attention shifts from physical to the online world, digital marketing has become bigger and more powerful than traditional advertising methods. Digital advertising spends in the US overtook traditional ads in 2019[1] and are projected to form more than two-thirds of all advertising expenditures in the US by the year 2023.[2] Google's global ad revenue for 2019 amounted to roughly USD 134.81 billion. This trend is merely a beginning for larger things to follow.

Closer home, the digital advertising industry in India surpassed print media to become #2 with INR 22,057 crores spends in the year 2019, according to a GroupM report[3]. Advertising spends on television remain on top, but digital is growing at a faster rate, expected to grow at 26% YoY compared to television's 10.7%.[4]

A typical Millennial has multiple social media accounts and uses more than one device to access these. With each social media profile accessed and webpage browsed, there is a bombardment of a slew of pop-ups, interstitials, banners, text and video ads, each one vying for a click-through. With the increasing use of advanced algorithms and technologies like Big Data, Artificial Intelligence and Machine Learning, marketers are trying to focus their marketing efforts sharper than ever before to deliver an ever-higher return on marketing spends.

Yet, as we saw in the Daniel Wellington case study, spending an exorbitant amount of money may neither be desirable nor advisable if marketers follow the principles and practices of FOMO marketing as detailed in this book.

With their distinct buying habits and increasing share of spending power, Millennials, as a segment deserve marketers' attention more than ever before. Growing up with cable television ads and exposed to a plethora of mediums, Millennials are weary and wary of traditional advertising. Capturing their increasingly shorter attention spans and persuading them to purchase from a brand will require more than just creative advertising.

Authenticity and relatability remain two pillars of any communication reaching out to Millennials. FOMO marketing seeks to integrate both of these and form a compelling pitch. FOMO marketing understands and puts to use the reality of Millennials' digital lives and uses the fear appeal as a marketer's tool to grab consumers' interest and expedite purchase decisions.

Another critical aspect of marketing today is developing contextualised approaches while showcasing or pitching a new product or service. As the Netflix case study shows, creating content and relevant buzzwords such as #Cokenomics with references to popular real-world phenomena can substantially boost consumers' interest in the message and consequently, the product or service. The crux of the strategy lies in engaging consumers through quality content they would like to consume rather than by aggressively feeding them with what brands want to convey.

Using this book as a guide to frame and implement marketing strategies can support emerging as well as established businesses in decoding and enthralling the Millennial customer.

As a marketer, it is time not to fear FOMO but to embrace it.

Notes

Chapter 1: Introduction

1. Patrick McGinnis, "Social Theory at HBS: McGinnis' Two FOs", The Harbus, May 10, 2004, https://harbus.org/2004/Social-Theory-at-HBS-2749/

2. "Meaning of FOMO in English", Lexico.com - Powered by Oxford, https://www.lexico.com/definition/fomo

Chapter 2: The Alchemy of FOMO

1. Madhav Chanchani, "Indians spent 4.3 hours a day on smartphones in March, up 24%", The Times of

India, April 17, 2020, http://timesofindia.indiatimes.com/articleshow/75192318.cms

2. "Distribution of Facebook users worldwide as of October 2020, by age and gender", Statista, October 2020, https://www.statista.com/statistics/376128/facebook-global-user-age-distribution/

3. "Facebook by the Numbers: Stats, Demographics & Fun Facts", Omnicore, October 28, 2020, https://www.omnicoreagency.com/facebook-statistics/

4. Gold J, Gold I. The "Truman Show" delusion: psychosis in the global village. Cogn Neuropsychiatry. 2012 Nov;17(6):455-72. doi: 10.1080/13546805.2012.666113. Epub 2012 May 29. PMID: 22640240.

5. "Ultimate Guide to Hashtags". Quick Sprout, February 24, 2019, https://www.quicksprout.com/ultimate-guide-to-hashtags/

6. Amandeep Dhir, Yossiri Yossatorn, Puneet Kaur, Sufen Chen, "Online social media fatigue and psychological wellbeing—A study of compulsive use, fear of missing out, fatigue, anxiety and depression", International Journal of Information Management, Volume 40, 2018, Pages 141-152, ISSN 0268-4012, https://doi.org/10.1016/j.ijinfomgt.2018.01.012 ,

http://www.sciencedirect.com/science/article/pii/S0268401217310629

Chapter 3: Millennials

1. Sheera Frenkel, Mike Isaac, Cecilia Kang and Gabriel J.X. Dance, "Facebook Employees Stage Virtual Walkout to Protest Trump Posts", The New York Times, June 1, 2020, https://www.nytimes.com/2020/06/01/technology/facebook-employee-protest-trump.html/

2. "Stress by generations: 2012." American Psychological Association, January 1, 2012, http://www.apa.org/news/press/releases/stress/2012/generations

Chapter 4: Selling Fear, FOMO Style

1. Dr Philip Kotler, "Dr. Philip Kotler Answers Your Questions on Marketing", https://kotlermarketing.com/phil_questions.shtml#answer3

2. Kahneman & Tversky, "Prospect theory", 1979 https://www.behavioraleconomics.com/resources/mini-encyclopedia-of-be/loss-aversion/

Chapter 5: Marketing to Millennials

1. Brand Keys, https://www.brandkeys.com/

Chapter 6: Crafting FOMO in Marketing Strategy

1. "Endowment Effect", Interaction Design Foundation, https://www.interaction-design.org/literature/topics/endowment-effect

Chapter 7: Case Studies: The Binge Trap – Netflix

1. Trevor Wheelwright, "Millennials Will Spend 13 Years Watching Netflix", HowtoWatch, September 23, 2019, https://www.howtowatch.com/millennials-will-spend-13-years-watching-netflix/

2. "Netflix Subscriber Growth 2x Expectations; Good News Or Peak?", Forbes, April 28, 2020, https://www.forbes.com/sites/greatspeculations/2020/04/28/netflix-subscriber-growth-2x-expectations-good-news-or-peak/

3. Jonathan Easton, "Netflix produced nine times more content than Amazon in 2019 with international expansion key", Digital TV Europe, March 18, 2020, https://www.digitaltveurope.com/2020/03/18/netflix-produced-nine-times-more-content-than-amazon-in-2019-with-international-expansion-key/

Influencer Marketing Strategy – Daniel Wellington

1. "Socialbakers Reports Brand-Sponsored Influencer Posts Surge by 150% on Instagram", Socialbakers, April 30, 2019, https://www.socialbakers.com/press-release/socialbakers-reports-brand-sponsored-influencer-posts-surge-by-150-on-instagram

Epilogue

1. Jasmine Enberg, "US Digital Ad Spending 2019", eMarketer, March 28, 2019, https://www.emarketer.com/content/us-digital-ad-spending-2019

2. Jacob Landis-Eigsti, "Online Advertising vs Traditional Advertising 2020: Digital Ads are King", Jacob LE Video Production, https://jacoblevideoproduction.com/digital-ads-have-surpassed-tv-ads-for-the-first-time-ever/

3. "Indian Ad Spends Estimated to Grow at 10.7% in 2020", GroupM, February 5, 2020, https://www.groupm.com/newsroom/indian-ad-spends-estimated-to-grow-at-10-7-in-2020-groupms-tyny-report/

4. Venkata Susmita Biswas, "Digital surpasses print to become 2nd largest advertising medium after TV",

Financial Express, February 6, 2020, https://www.financialexpress.com/industry/technology/digital-surpasses-print-to-become-2nd-largest-advertising-medium-after-tv/1857934/

About the Author

Sumeet Singh Lamba is a Senior Marketing Professional with one of the leading telecommunications brands in India. Being a domain expert with over 13 years of experience across various multinational groups and brands, Sumeet understands consumer behaviour, motivation, and what drives conversions. With hands-on experience in attracting, acquiring, and retaining customers, Sumeet has employed his deep understanding of consumers' psyche to craft and execute hugely successful marketing campaigns.

A postgraduate in management from one of the leading B-Schools in India, Sumeet is currently pursuing a doctorate in business management.

Born a digital native, Sumeet was naturally inclined to the networked reality and become a whizz-kid at the age of 16. In the year 2000, he developed India's first meta-search engine, HumHaiIndia.com, later renamed Tazaa.com for which he was widely covered in the Indian media. Being a millennial himself and a techie at heart, he understands and relates easily to his target audience, whether in the real world or online.

In his first book, *FOMO: Marketing to Millennials*, Sumeet deals with the concept of 'Fear of Missing Out' or FOMO as experienced by modern-day consumers. He endeavours to give an insight into this aspect of consumer behaviour among millennials, opening up newer dimensions for marketers across industries and in a variety of settings. The book provides a practical approach to utilise FOMO as a marketing technique for various campaigns and brand placement appealing to such consumers.

About the Author

Find out more about the author on
www.sumeetlamba.com
or connect with him **@sumeetlamba**
on Facebook, Twitter, Instagram and LinkedIn.

Printed in Poland
by Amazon Fulfillment
Poland Sp. z o.o., Wrocław